At Home with Diana

Also by Deb Stratas

Diana, A Spencer in Love

Diana, A Spencer in Turmoil

Diana, A Spencer Forever

At Home with Diana

by Deb Stratas

At Home with Diana

Author: Deb Stratas
Website: debstratas.com
Editor: Robin Djokoto
Cover Art: Katrina Robert

ISBN: 9781790828999

Acknowledgments

At Home with Diana is dedicated to everyone who loved or still loves the late Diana, Princess of Wales. This book is a companion to my *Diana Spencer trilogy*, to give you added insight into the homes that were the backdrop to Diana's incredible life.

In researching this book, I've personally toured every English and Scottish home Diana lived in, including her holiday residences. I also mined 60+ Diana biographies to examine her experiences and relationships. I'd like to thank everyone who has contributed to this impressive body of research as it helped me immensely in bringing Diana's story to life.

I'd especially like to thank all the people who warmly welcomed me into their homes and cities across Scotland and England. Everyone was extremely kind and helpful during my research trips from Canada. Special thanks to Jeremy, Neil and Sheila, Sheila and her son from Aberdeen, Elisa & Jacopo, Lyndsey & Miles, and Jeannie. I couldn't have done it without you!

Table of Contents

Author's Preface

Park House

Althorp Estate

Coleherne Court

Clarence House

Buckingham Palace

The Royal Yacht Britannia

Balmoral Castle

Sandringham House

Highgrove House

Kensington Palace

Spencer House

Preface

Diana, Princess of Wales was a fascinating, vulnerable, beautiful, compassionate and complex woman. Even two decades and counting after her tragic death, she captivates our attention. We still long to know her, what motivated her, why she made some of the choices she did, and how she managed to make such a huge impact on the world in her short life.

At Home with Diana explores her story from the perspective of where and how she lived her life. From her birth at Park House on July 1, 1961 to her death from her final home at Kensington Palace on August 31, 1997 – her houses tell a meaningful part of the story of how Diana lived. Always wealthy, Diana was privileged to reside in some of the most famous and sumptuous homes and palaces in the world.

As part of my research for the book, I've personally visited all of Diana's homes. It was a moving adventure walking the halls that the Princess walked, and feeling her spirit in the places that brought her joy and despair. If you haven't visited the U.K., I strongly recommend you make the trip. Most of the residences are open part or all of the year. Most of them are within a couple of hours of London where you can start your own Diana journey. To get the most out of all these royal residences, I've also shared my personal experiences visiting them, along with a few tips.

Take Diana's journey from her 1961 birth to her tragic death in 1997 – just thirty-six short years. Learn fascinating facts about what it was like to live and holiday in each of her incredible homes, as her life unfolded. You'll read her story as she blossoms from a young woman to a royal bride, Princess of Wales, loving mother and world icon.

I've enhanced Diana's story with the history of each of these special houses. I've included a photo of each home as well as some from my personal tours. Besides a comprehensive review of Diana's story, I've added highlights of her life that she experienced in each residence. And I have provided relevant advice and links about visiting each home today. Note that opening times and exhibits may change so be sure to check and plan ahead to avoid disappointment. It's frustrating to travel to a highly anticipated location to find it just about to close! And although you'll be eager with anticipation when you see the size of these large homes, remember that only a few state and public rooms are typically open to the public. You won't see any bedrooms or private family areas.

Although I've researched all these residences extensively and consider myself a Princess Diana storyteller, these are *my* personal observations, opinions and discoveries about Diana's life. I hope you enjoy and gain some new perspectives about our beloved and much-missed Diana, Princess of Wales.

ONE

Park House

Sandringham Estate, Norfolk, England
(1961 – 1975)

Diana Frances Spencer was born on July 1, 1961 in her parent's bedroom at Park House in Norfolk. Neighboring the Queen's Sandringham Estate, Park House was a sprawling family home where Viscount Johnnie Spencer and his wife Frances had lived since the early days of their marriage. Park House was built in 1863 at the request of then-Prince of Wales (later Edward VII). In the 1930s, King George V leased Park House to his friend Edmund Roche, 4th Baron Fermoy. Baron Fermoy and his wife (later a Woman of the Bedchamber and close confidante to The

1

Queen Mother), had three children born at Park House, including daughter Frances in 1936. Frances, of course, was Diana's mother. She was born January 20, 1936, the same day King George V died at Sandringham House.

Upon Frances' marriage to John Spencer, Viscount Althorp in 1954, the couple took over the lease on Park House from her parents. Diana, her older sisters Sarah and Jane, and her younger brother Charles were all born on this family estate. An infant son John had been born in 1960 but lived less than a day, and was buried at Sandringham.

Diana was the third girl born to Johnnie and Francis. Although not a disappointment in herself, the fact that she was not a boy and thus the Spencer heir, was a bitter blow to both parents. She wasn't even named for a week, as her parents Johnnie and Frances had been certain she'd be the longed-for son.

Park House was a large farmhouse originally used for overflow guests at nearby royal Sandringham Estate. Sandringham is used by the royal family for annual Christmas and Easter celebrations. Her Majesty, the Queen lives in Buckingham Palace and Windsor Castle for most of the year. The entire family convenes at the Balmoral Estate in Scotland for a two-month holiday each August and September. The royal schedule rarely varies and hasn't for generations.

Diana's nearest neighbors were rarely in residence when she was a child. She did see them from time-to-time and was comfortable in the royal presence. After all, the Spencers had been a premier British aristocratic family since the 1700's.

Diana and Prince Andrew were closest in age (he was a year older than her), so she spent more time playing with him and his younger brother Edward than the dashing but often absent Prince Charles. Many expected the young Diana might marry into the royal family someday – but she and Andrew never became more than just good friends. In fact, she eventually followed in her mother's own footsteps by marrying a man twelve years her senior – just as Frances had done. Although Diana married a Prince, while her mother settled on a Viscount with prospects of becoming an Earl someday.

The ten-bedroom Victorian Park House estate was large and had a nondescript sand-brick exterior. Staff cottages, outbuildings, stables and a tennis court dotted the property. The children's outdoor playhouse sported a windmill atop the roof. A brick wall separated the home from its Sandringham neighbor. On the Queen's side of the wall was the graveyard where the infant John Spencer was buried.

Inside the home was a comfortable, if not formal layout. It was more a collection of reception rooms, a formal drawing room where Frances' mother had once given piano concerts, and smaller rooms scattered around the main floor. The style of furnishings and artwork was predominantly Victorian, with dark, heavy furniture and portraits of royalty and local hunting scenes covering the walls.

The large nineteenth-century country kitchen had stone-flagged floors and a hearth. A pre-World War I stove (or aga) dominated the space. It was the domain of Mrs. Smith, the Spencer's housekeeper and wife of the Park House butler. It was in this kitchen that Diana first adopted her habit of dropping by staff quarters to chat with cooks, maids and other household employees. She thought nothing of popping in, talking and giggling with any staff that were on hand, and helping herself to snacks in the process.

Next to the kitchen was the schoolroom (a converted butler's pantry) which was used for home schooling the Spencer daughters. Gertrude Allen, nicknamed Ally, was the girls' governess, and presided over the mini-classroom until the children were ready for boarding school.

The second floor housed all the adult bedrooms and bathrooms. The nursery floor occupied the entire third floor, often known as the attics. The Spencer children spent many happy hours here in their early childhood days.

Childhood at Park House was the epitome of English country life. Playing in the nursery or on the vast grounds was encouraged, and the children ran free as Frances battled post-partum depression, and their father pursued his own country interests.

Once the much-needed male heir was born in 1964, the Spencer marriage began to disintegrate. At only twenty-eight, Frances was bored and restless with rural life – and her husband. Although their wedding had been attended by many members of the royal family and seen as a glamourous society occasion, the Viscount and his wife didn't have much in common. They entertained little, as Johnnie spent most of his time supervising the estate from his study or out on horseback.

There have been many rumors about darker aspects of the Spencer marriage. I will say only that these rumors include serious drinking on the parts of both Johnnie and Frances, and possible domestic violence between them. None these rumors have been officially documented or proven. However, if true, this could explain a lot about Diana's later insecurities, feelings of abandonment, and struggles with the eating disorder bulimia. At this point, all I can say with certainty is that the Spencer marriage grew troubled at this time, and tensions filled Park House.

When Diana was just six years old, Frances infamously "bolted" and left her husband and small family. The truth is far different than this widespread story. Frances *was* spending more and more time in London. She had met the then-married Peter Shand-Kydd, a wallpaper magnate, and fallen in love with him. Sarah and Jane were away at West Heath boarding school, and Diana was heartbroken to be without her sisters.

Initially, Frances had decided to leave Johnnie and had taken a flat in London. She had enrolled both Diana and her brother Charles in local day schools and planned to have them with her in the Cadogan Place apartment. The two youngest Spencers stayed with their mother in London and visited their father at weekends. At this point, the separation was tense but not acrimonious. All this changed Christmas 1968.

Frances and Johnnie had decided to spend the holiday together with all the children at Park House. At the end of the strained break, Frances tried to leave with the younger children. Unexpectedly and quite firmly, Johnnie refused to let them go with their mother. Frances was dazed and bewildered but departed without them.

From then on, Diana and Charles spent weekends and various holidays with their mother but lived permanently with Viscount Spencer at the country estate. Children are resilient and soon got used to the new arrangement, although the partings from Frances were always tearful and pain-filled.

Diana later recalled being frightened and lonely at night in the nursery, wanting to call out to a mother who wasn't there. She longed to comfort Charles when he cried out, but was too scared to leave her bed to go to her brother.

A series of nannies came and went at Park House. Those that the children didn't like they forced to flee by playing vicious pranks on them. Throwing clothes out the nursery window, locking them in bathrooms, and filling chair cushions with pins were some of their favorite tricks to drive away unpopular new nannies. Johnnie remained distant and remote with his youngest children.

Just when things couldn't get any worse, the divorce proceedings began. Frances expected to get full custody of the four children as was customary in England at the time. However, she hadn't counted on Johnnie's determination – and the establishment - to keep them. He even enlisted the help of Frances' mother – Lady Ruth Fermoy – to testify against her own daughter! As a close staff member serving the Queen Mother, she was appalled at the shame and embarrassment brought on the family by her wayward daughter. In the end, the establishment was all too much, and Frances lost custody of her children. I expect she probably never got over this crushing blow, although she did keep in lifelong communication with all her children and saw them often. She never forgave her own mother for this ultimate betrayal.

After the divorce, Diana and Charles were enrolled in a local day school called Silfield. Varying reports cite Diana as either extraverted and bubbly, or shy and withdrawn. Perhaps these moods related to the events occurring at her two different homes as she tried to cope with the ever-changing reality of her life.

After the divorce, Frances married Peter Shand-Kydd and they enjoyed their London life. By all accounts, he was a nice man and well-liked by the Spencer children.

At age nine, Diana was sent to Riddlesworth boarding school. She hated being separated from her brother Charlie as she had become a surrogate mother to him, and worried how he would manage without her. But she had no choice.

After a settling-in period, Diana began to enjoy life at Riddlesworth. Although not scholarly, she loved sports – especially swimming; and learned to play the piano. She found her true passion for dancing here, and eagerly took up both tap and ballet lessons. Upon returning home at a school break, she was delighted to find her father had installed a swimming pool. She spent many hours swimming and perfecting her perfect dives – always eager for an approving audience.

In due course, she graduated from Riddlesworth and went off to West Heath, where her sister Jane was still a student. At twelve years old, Diana was already 5' 10" and had to give up on her dream of becoming a professional ballerina. She was popular with the other girls, but was still shy at times. She was becoming a pretty young woman, although even then had a habit of ducking her head and blushing when embarrassed or uncomfortable. She had brought many of her stuffed animals with her, a habit that she would maintain for a lifetime. She met Carolyn Pride who would also become a long-time confidante, room-mate and dear friend.

It was at West Heath that Diana first started to perform charity work, which she took to quickly and naturally. She loved to volunteer at the local home for handicapped children, and the psychiatric hospital. While the other girls balked at this uncomfortable community service, Diana embraced it, and loved to bring smiles to the faces of those less fortunate.

She also became quite domesticated and loved cleaning, organizing and even garden weeding. She kept her clothes immaculate and took great pride in her appearance. Although no eating disorders were reported from these school days, some have said that at times she loved to gorge on sweets or eat large quantities of food when dared.

As a teen, Diana's romantic streak took hold. She loved to read and spent many hours with her nose in romantic novels where the dashing hero saved the maiden in distress, and lived happily ever after.

Diana's favorite memories came from the reunions when all four Spencer children returned to Norfolk. They all loved Park House, and spending time together.

All this changed in 1975, when Earl Jack Spencer died. Diana's father now became the 8th Earl Spencer, and with the earldom came a major move to Althorp – the Spencer estate in Northamptonshire, England. Diana was fourteen years old.

Significant Events that happened at Park House

- Lady Diana Frances Spencer's birth: 1961
- Birth of future 9th Earl Spencer, Charles Edward Maurice Spencer: 1964
- Separation of Viscount and Lady John Spencer: 1967
- Viscount and Lady Spencer divorce finalized: 1969
- Frances Spencer marries Peter Shand-Kydd: 1969
- Diana leaves for Riddlesworth Boarding School: 1970
- Diana's grandmother, Countess Cynthia Spencer dies at the age of 75: 1972
- 7th Earl Spencer dies, Viscount Johnnie Spencer becomes 8th Earl Spencer, family moves to Althorp House: 1975

In Her Own Words

"It was endlessly explorable and filled with wonderful memories of so many pranks. I can see myself now, seated on the nursery floor, playing with my toys, totally into my own thing." Diana, Princess of Wales.

Park House Today

Park House is truly right next door to the Sandringham Estate. You can still enter the curved driveway and look up at Diana's first home. It is welcoming and warm, with lots of trees, shrubs and wildflowers along the lane.

I took the train to King's Lynn to visit both Park House and

---

the Sandringham Estate. The train station seems timeless and unchanged since Diana and her brother Charles took the train regularly to visit their mother in London. I could just imagine young Diana asking her nanny for a packet of crisps for the train in the little tea shop.

King's Lynn Train Station

I had a lovely cup of tea and biscuit here as I waited for the train to London, much as Diana likely did decades ago. It was surreal to say the least!

This station still has a royal connection. The Queen takes the train from London just before Christmas each year for the family holiday at Sandringham. After the two-hour train journey, she's whisked by limo to Sandringham.

Park House has been converted to the Park House Hotel, a respite retreat which is not open to the public. It provides holidays for disabled people and their caregivers. How fitting for Diana's childhood home to provide sanctuary to those in need! parkhousehotel.org.uk

TWO

Althorp Estate

Northamptonshire, England
(1975 – 1978)

The move to Althorp Estate was not a happy one for Diana and her siblings. They loved Park House, had grown up there and were leaving behind childhood friends. At the age of fourteen, Diana was away at boarding school most of the time, and never truly considered Althorp a home.

The Spencer children were familiar with Althorp, of course. They had visited it several times to see their grandparents, Earl Jack Spencer and his wife and Countess, Cynthia. Diana loved her grandmother dearly and had been heartbroken when she died in 1972. She hadn't been to Althorp since her grandmother's death, and the house felt like a museum without her. Diana closely resembled Cynthia physically, and felt a powerful connection to this gentle lady. Even later in life, Diana remarked that she believed her grandmother was looking down on her from heaven and protecting her.

Johnnie's relationship with his father was completely different. The two did not get along, the old Earl being disappointed in his less than ambitious and amiable son Johnnie. Jack was a gruff, no nonsense sort of man; and an avid art collector and curator. He took great pride in the estate and possessions of Althorp and spent his life maintaining, cataloguing and showcasing his vast works of art – paintings and sculptures. Johnnie was more enamored of farming and rural life and raising his young family at Park House. So, the young Spencers had not spent much time at the vast Althorp Estate.

When their father became the new Earl Spencer, Charles became Viscount and the sisters became Ladies. From here was born Lady Diana Spencer.

Undoubtedly part of the children's' negative association with Althorp House was Johnnie's acquisition of a new wife – the former Countess Raine Dartmouth. "Acid Raine" as she was soon dubbed, was a flamboyant socialite, mother of four, community activist and the daughter of the famous romance novelist, Barbara Cartland. Diana obsessively read Cartland's books and built her image of a storybook "happily ever after" from these types of fiction. Raine and the Earl fell passionately in love, married privately, and by all accounts had a successful marriage.

However, the Spencer children hated their new stepmother on sight, and were merciless in their derision, taunting and distaste for her. Poor Raine – she tried so hard to win the approval of the three sisters and future

Earl, but to no avail. From ignoring her completely to outward criticism and rejection, the new Countess could do no right.

It didn't help that with Althorp came exorbitant inheritance taxes, and a property that needed major maintenance and attention. The indomitable Raine (under Johnnie's benevolent watch) sold many valuable pieces of artwork, fired lifelong staff, and even opened up Althorp to the public for paying tours. Besides paintings, furniture and priceless porcelains, there was also silver and gold, original Beethoven and Mozart manuscripts, drawings, rare books and properties – a vast treasure trove from which Raine sold over the years. None of these actions endeared the Spencer children to the new lady of the manor, but all these measures were, in fact, necessary to save the estate and fund the much-needed maintenance and long-neglected repairs.

"Come along, Johnnie." Raine strove to move the tour along a little faster. "At this rate, we won't get to the drawing room until teatime." The Countess fussed over her husband.

"Yes, dear," the Earl responded meekly. "Let's show Nora the splendid job you've done on the South Drawing Room."

Another glance passed between Diana and her brother, but no one said a word.

Nora gasped again as she entered the South Drawing Room, but this time it was a gasp of horror. The room resembled a brothel more than a drawing room. The walls were covered with dark-red brocade wallpaper which matched the heavy draperies. The room was gilt from ceiling to floor with gold ceiling fixtures, lighting, fireplace decoration and on any other surface you could imagine. Large, ostentatious bouquets of flowers stood on every available surface.

"Do you like it, dear?" asked Raine with delight. "This room was so cluttered before I took over. I've removed some of the

paintings and redecorated to make it more modern." The Countess beamed. From Diana, A Spencer in Love.

Althorp House is the Spencer ancestral estate of 13,000 acres in Northamptonshire, England. The mansion dates to 1508 when it was purchased by the first Earl Spencer, a sheep farmer with vast holdings. The name Althorp is derived from possible older names like "Oldthorpe," "Ollethorpe," "Holtropp," and "Aldrop." When I visited the estate, I asked if the proper pronunciation is Althorp or "Altrupp" – the guide confirmed Althorp which was a bit surprising given my research. I think perhaps the current Spencers got tired of correcting people, and have accepted the most common pronunciation.

The house at Althorp started out as a beautiful red brick Tudor building, but its appearance was radically altered over time to change the exterior brick, add columns and expand the outbuildings extensively. The estate is over 100,000 square feet in total. There are 600+ world-class paintings in the home and 3,000 First Editions in the Library. Imagine a home with thirty-one bedrooms and eighty-eight fireplaces!

Two of Diana's most famous female Spencer ancestors were Sarah, the Duchess of Marlborough who was a close confidante of Queen Anne before a massive falling out; and Georgiana Cavendish, the Duchess of Devonshire. Diana certainly came from a long line of strong Spencer women!

The Great Dining Room in the east wing extension of the house was added in 1877, its walls hung with faded, red damask silk. Numerous fireplaces and furnishings were brought to Althorp from Spencer House in London during The Blitz in World War II for safekeeping, and remain to this day. The Picture Gallery stretches for 115 feet on the first floor of the west wing, and is home to one of Europe's finest collections of paintings and sculptures.

Entering Althorp, guests are enthralled by the formal Wootten Hall – a large entranceway spanning two stories; adorned with priceless portraits and paintings. The black and white marble checked floor is striking. Young Diana was known to slip down here many times in the middle of the night to practice her dancing.

The main floor also boasts a Saloon, formal Dining Room (meant to mirror the design of the one at Buckingham Palace), several Reception, Drawing and Sitting rooms, a Billiards Room, and several other jaw-dropping formal rooms. In all, there are over 90 rooms in the house. Of course, there is a large, bustling kitchen (a place where Diana would sneak down to for between-meal snacks and chats), and staff quarters.

The Picture Gallery is virtually unchanged over the centuries with gleaming oak floors, paneled walls, nineteen-foot high ceilings and some of the greatest masterpieces found in the UK. There is Van Dyck's *War and Peace,* and royal portraits of James I, Charles II, Lady Jane Grey, and dozens of other breath-taking paintings. There is even a secret, tiny door cut into the oak paneling that leads to an upper staircase – supposedly visited by "the girl in the grey slippers" – a ghostly figure seen by an elderly aunt many years ago. There is also rumor of a male apparition – a 19th-century groom who has been seen to go around the house late at night checking that all the candles have been safely snuffed out. How exciting!

The upper floor houses many bedrooms, some themed (e.g. The Oak Bedroom), and all filled with beautiful, rare and stunning antiques and art pieces. The Oak Bedroom was the famous location where John Spencer - the first Earl Spencer – married his sweetheart in secret. This was a love match between John and Georgiana Poyntz who were scheduled to be married at John's coming-of-age Christmas festivities in 1755. A large party of 400 guests stayed at the estate enjoying parties and balls leading up to the Christmas Day wedding. The groom, however had other plans – he surprised his shy bride with a private wedding in the Oak Bedroom on December 20th. The newly wedded couple were then presented to the company already married. It would turn out to be a happy relationship as the couple split their time between Althorp and their London home – Spencer House. I'm sure Diana found this quite romantic and seeded her own desire for a romantic and fairy tale marriage from this Spencer love story.

Her Althorp room was on the first floor – the old night nursery – and her bed-full of soft toys were transported from Park House to her new home.

Raine had decorated Diana's room in what she thought a young teen would love: twin beds, white-painted furniture, a flowered couch and bookshelves. From the window near her bed, Diana could look out onto the grass and lily pond. But she felt uncomfortable and isolated – except for weekends when the house was open to visitors.

Diana missed the familiarity and warmth of Park House. She always considered herself a "Norfolk person" and found Althorp remote. A small but welcome consolation was the swimming pool that the new Earl had built on the property. Diana spent many hours diving and swimming. She also liked rowing out to the tiny island in the middle of the Round Oval lake to the rear of the house – either to read and sunbathe or gather greenery for the housekeeper's flowers. She always went alone and took solace in the privacy of the idyllic setting. I'm sure this memory is what led Diana's brother Charles to the decision to bury his sister here many years later. Finally, a resting place of peace and solitude.

In total, the grounds of Althorp estate contain twenty-eight listed buildings and structures, including staff quarters, stable block, hunting grounds, and swimming pool.

Once the awkward move to Althorp was made, the children scattered back to their respective boarding schools, except for Sarah who was old enough to live with a room-mate in a London flat. Diana couldn't wait to join her there when she was old enough.

In 1978, Johnnie suffered a severe stroke and almost died. Diana would later claim that she had a premonition that her father would fall gravely ill, and if he didn't die immediately, would survive. This proved to be true, although he was critically ill for months. His bride Raine supervised his recovery, and even arranged for a trial drug from Germany for him. It saved his life although he was permanently weakened.

During this trying illness, relations between the Countess and the Spencer children went from bad to worse. Raine kept the children from seeing their father in hospital, and they took to sneaking in after hours when Raine briefly left the Earl's bedside. Although she nursed him back from the brink of death, the Spencer children never seemed to appreciate what Raine had done. Somehow, she could never win against their love and loyalty for "darling daddy."

It has been well documented that Diana finished her school career with no official credentials except for pet-caring medals and diving trophies. It's true that she sat her "O-level" (for ordinary) exams twice, and failed them both times. This would be the equivalent of a high school diploma covering such subjects as English, Math, History and Geography. Young Diana took this hard and it was the basis for her life-long insecurity about being "thick as a plank" or having a "brain the size of a pea." I personally think Diana was highly intelligent, proved later to be a quick learner, and was astounding at reading and empathizing with people. However, she felt inferior to many academic and accomplished people she would later meet – including the finely-educated and well-read Prince Charles.

His Royal Highness, the Prince of Wales visited Althorp in 1977 for a dinner party while dating Diana's sister Sarah. Diana was only sixteen at the time and probably blushed and gushed her way through the initial meeting in true teenage style. The dashing Prince asked young Diana to show him Althorp's famous Picture Gallery, but clever Sarah interceded and took over the tour. But the first spark of romance was ignited at Diana's teenage Althorp home.

After finishing with boarding school for good, Diana's parents were rather unsure what to do with this sixteen-year old girl. She was definitely not on an academic track and was too young to join her sisters in London. So, it was decided to send her to a finishing school in Switzerland called Institut Alpin Vidamanette.

Although Diana made friends at the elite school, she hated being forced to only speak French, and was fairly hopeless at cooking school. She did learn how to ski, so it wasn't a complete waste of time, but Diana was bored and unhappy. She spent just one term there, and wrote countless letters to her parents, sisters, and even her Grandmother Fermoy begging to be allowed to come home. Johnnie and Frances finally relented, and Diana packed her trunk and came home to Althorp. Her school days were now truly over.

In March of 1978, Diana's older sister Jane married Robert Fellowes, then assistant private secretary to the Queen. Diana was a bridesmaid at their Westminster Abbey nuptials. After the wedding, Diana came home to Althorp but was again restless and bored, longing to take up the single girl life in London. Diana chafed to escape from the cloying and domineering Raine and was finally allowed – at the age of seventeen – to come to London to stay in her mother's flat.

Diana never lived at Althorp again, although she visited it intermittently throughout her life. After her divorce from Prince Charles she had hoped to move to the Garden House on the Althorp property, but her brother Charles as the new Earl refused her request, citing publicity and security issues. He offered her other properties which she refused. Diana never forgave him for not providing a safe haven for herself and her boys; and the brother and sister were on strained relations for the rest of her life.

Significant Events that happened at Althorp House

- Spencer family moves from Park House to Althorp: 1975
- Earl Spencer marries Raine, Countess of Dartmouth: 1976
- Diana leaves school with no "O" level exams passed: 1977
- Earl Spencer suffers a massive stroke: 1978
- Diana goes to Finishing School: 1978
- Diana moves to London: 1978

In Her Own Words

"When I was thirteen, we moved to Althorp in Northampton and that was a terrible wrench, leaving Norfolk, because that's where everybody I'd grown up with lived. We had to move because Grandfather died, and life took a very big turn because my stepmother Raine appeared on the scene. We all hated her so much because we thought she was going to take Daddy away from us." Diana, Princess of Wales

Althorp Today:

The Althorp Estate is open to visitors each summer (July – September.) Food & Drink and Literary Festivals are also held annually.

I highly recommend a visit to Althorp. It takes some planning as it's a couple of hours outside of London. You'll need to take the train and taxi, or arrange local transportation, but it's well worth it.

I'm forever grateful to my Welsh taxi driver Jeremy who rescued me from London tube problems to deliver me to Althorp on time for my scheduled visit in the summer of 2018. He patiently waited three hours for me to explore the estate fully before returning me safely to London. He's now become a dear friend and supporter of my books. Email him at jeremycab@icloud.com if you need a ride in London!

As you enter the gates, you'll be reminded of Diana's death – the place where the first flower bouquets were laid when the world heard of her tragic death; and the final scene of the hearse bearing her coffin disappearing forever. The current Earl Spencer has planted a beautiful set of thirty-six oak trees that line the driveway – one for each year of Diana's life. It's hoped that in years to come the trees will grow together overhead to form a joined arbor. Hundreds of white roses and water lilies were also planted in the Princess's honor. It's a lovely walk down the drive to the stable block, with the house beyond it.

You can enjoy a lovely tea and scone in the redesigned stable block which is arranged in a quadrangle with outdoor seating. There's also a small museum and gift shop. View an entire bookcase wall of condolence books sent to Diana's family from all over the world. See the original paper draft of Earl Spencer's powerful eulogy for his sister, along with other Spencer artifacts.

The house itself is magnificent and full of Diana memories. The portrait of her that was displayed on the landing of Kensington Palace now hangs in the Great Hall. There are tour guides throughout the building who are friendly and knowledgeable.

Of course, the highlight is the Oval Lake and island. Diana is buried on the center island, which is inaccessible to visitors. The lake is a short walk from the house, scenic and peaceful. You can wander around the perimeter of the entire island and quietly reflect on the benches that dot the area. There is also a monument to Diana at the far end where people still leave flowers and notes.

Being able to pay respects to Princess Diana at her final resting place is a moving experience that shouldn't be missed. Plan to spend at least three to four hours at the estate to see and experience it all. Check spencerofalthorp.com for opening times and visitor information.

Oval Lake

Diana Monument

THREE

Coleherne Court

London, England
(1979 – 1981)

In the summer of 1978, just after her seventeenth birthday, Diana moved to London. She wanted to room with her sister Sarah, but the older Spencer resisted having the blossoming Diana cramp her style, so she refused to become flat-mates with her. Diana enrolled in a cookery school at Wimbledon while she stayed at Cadogan Place with her mother and step-father. It was from here that she commuted back and forth to the hospital when her father had his stroke.

Diana did odd cleaning and babysitting jobs to make ends meet. For a girl in her advantaged position, it was either that or a secretarial post, and she wasn't at all interested in an office job. She also cleaned and ironed for her sister Sarah for a paltry wage, but as she adored both her sister and cleaning, she never complained

In November, she was invited with Sarah to Prince Charles' 30th birthday party at Buckingham Palace. It was the first time for Diana to dress up in a ball gown that she dieted to fit into; and she was excited but not intimidated by "Buck House." Charles remembered her from Althorp and commented that she'd "grown" since he'd last seen her. She murmured that she hoped not, and they shared a laugh. I'm sure she was thrilled to see the charming Prince again – even on the arm of her sister.

The romance between HRH, Prince Charles and Lady Sarah Spencer was starting to decline. Sarah had made a fatal blunder by telling the press that she "would only marry for love – whether it be the dustman or the Prince of Wales." The relationship had already been under strain due to Charles' busy schedule and Sarah's eating disorder anorexia nervosa. But speaking out so bluntly and publicly to the press was Sarah's undoing. The relationship was over – leaving the way clear for the younger Spencer sister – Diana.

On Diana's eighteenth birthday, she received an inheritance from her great-grandmother Frances Work. This gave her the means to buy her own London flat for about 60,000 pounds and truly start her independent life. Her mother Frances helped her decorate the three-bedroom Coleherne Court flat, and Diana promptly took in flat-mates to help pay the rent. After a bit of churn, Carolyn Pride, Virginia Pitman and Anne Bolton moved in and the four became fast friends. Diana was always in charge and made the housework schedule to ensure everyone did their share of cleaning and cooking.

Coleherne Court is located between Chelsea and South Kensington in London. It's a red brick and stone mansion block built in the early 1900's. The old Coleherne Court had been around when Brompton Lane, later the Old Brompton Road, curved through fields, nurseries and market gardens punctuated by cottages and large houses all the way to Brompton Road.

There has been a house at this location as far back as the 1600's. Ownership seems to have changed frequently. Among many others, the infamous poet and eminent doctor Sir Richard Blackmore lived here in the early 1700's. At one time, it was even a women's cycling club. The famous children's author Beatrix Potter lived nearby at Bolton Gardens.

Housing 213 luxury apartments, the building spans three blocks and is set in an acre of private landscaped gardens. For a short time when she lived here, Diana worked as a ballet teacher at Madame Vacani's dance studio but quit after a leg injury.

Through her sister Jane in 1979, she was put in contact with Kay Seth-Smith who ran the Young England Kindergarten School in Pimlico. Kay was instantly impressed with Diana's natural ease with pre-school children and she was hired as a teacher's assistant to work three days a week.

Diana thrived in this environment and loved teaching the toddlers drawing and dancing, as well as assisting with play times. She had a natural affinity for the youngsters; she giggled and laughed along with them.

It was also at this time that she started working two days a week as a part-time nanny for an American child, Patrick Robertson. His parents were on assignment from the U.S. to London, and mom Mary needed someone to look after one-year old Patrick while she worked at a London bank. Through the school, Diana was recommended, and after a warm and relaxed interview, was hired almost on-the-spot. She adored Patrick and he loved her right back. Diana also struck up a casual friendship with Mrs. Robertson – a relationship that lasted till the end of Diana's life.

This was a happy time for Diana – perhaps the happiest in her life. She was independent and living in one of the most exciting cities in the world – London. She loved her two jobs and had a busy and active social life. As a "Sloane Ranger," Diana was a stereotypical young upper-class young lady who pursued a distinctive fashionable lifestyle. The term stems from the Chelsea location where many of these wealthy young women lived and worked. Most came from privileged or titled backgrounds, had plenty of family money and didn't need to work. They were looking for men of equal or better status to marry and retire to the country with – to host dinner parties and fashionable weekends; and raise children and dogs. This was about the extent of Diana's ambitions as well, although Prince Charles had certainly caught her eye by now.

Diana dated casually throughout this time, but never got serious with any of the eligible young men who formed her set.

Life changed dramatically for Diana in July 1980 when she received an invitation from an acquaintance Philip De Pass to join him for a weekend party in West Sussex. He had informed her that the Prince of Wales would be attending, and Diana eagerly accepted the invitation.

At Petworth House, Diana joined the others as they watched the Prince play polo and then relaxed together over an outdoor barbecue. It was here that Diana approached the Prince and expressed her condolences about the loss of his dear great-uncle Lord Mountbatten who had been killed in an IRA boating attack the previous year.

The Prince had been devastated by the loss of his mentor, counsellor, pseudo grandfather and dear friend. Charles had been extremely close to his great-uncle and had sorely mourned his loss. He surely must have been shocked when young Diana (twelve years his junior) empathized with his loss and showed real concern for the Prince. As a fresh-faced, lovely and sincere eighteen-year old, Diana must have been irresistible to the ready-to-be married Prince of Wales.

After this encounter, the royal romance began in earnest. Diana was invited to the opera with Charles and their two grandmothers – Queen Elizabeth, the Queen Mother (Queen Mum), and her Lady of the Bedchamber, Lady Ruth Fermoy. Some believe it was the two grandmothers who played cupid to Charles and Diana. Charles was extremely close to his grandmother, and certainly would have listened to her advice. He was also a full-grown thirty-two-year-old man with mature likes and dislikes, and could certainly make up his own mind.

"Quick, quick. I have to meet Charles in twenty minutes." Diana's frantic tone greeted Carolyn as she came home to Coleherne Court the following Friday night. Carolyn helped Diana to wash and dry her hair, and dash on a quick makeup's application. "The pink or the navy?" Diana queried breathlessly as she pointed to two evening gowns rustled up by her two other flatmates. "He's taking me and my grandmother to Verdi's Requiem. He apologized for the last-minute invitation, but he

just realised it was the Verdi and thought I'd like to go. Isn't that thoughtful?"

"Definitely the pink, Duch," replied Carolyn thinking to herself it would have been more thoughtful if the Prince had given her friend more than twenty minutes' notice. From Diana, A Spencer in Love.

In any event, Charles was smitten with the lovely Lady Diana Spencer, and the two spent a lot of time together over the summer. She was twice invited up to the Scottish vacation estate of Balmoral, where she was introduced to the royal holiday activities of fishing, hunting, riding and long walks. Diana rarely rode due to a lifelong fear that stemmed from a childhood fall. The couple visited the weekend homes of many of Charles's friends – including Andrew and Camilla Parker-Bowles. She was even invited to spend Cowes Week with him and his entourage aboard the royal ship Britannia.

As Diana was falling in love with Charles, the press and paparazzi fell in love with her. Once the reporters and photographers of Fleet Street discovered her, Diana was followed and hounded day and night. She was stalked outside Coleherne Court, the phone rang off the hook with press tying to vie for statements, and Diana couldn't go anywhere without her picture being taken.

Diana had learned from her sister's mistake and never once cracked under the pressure or said anything controversial to the press. She became known as "Shy Di" because of her habit of blushing and ducking her head to avoid being photographed. Her enigmatic smile was captured on all the front pages of newspapers in the U.K. and around the world.

Diana was forced to deal with all this media scrutiny on her own. Because she was just a girlfriend of the Prince (and not yet a fiancé or wife), she was not entitled to royal protection coverage. And I'm sure the Queen and palace courtiers were astounded and shocked by all this attention placed on a seemingly nondescript nineteen-year-old aristocratic girl.

During the courtship, Diana and her flat-mates employed many techniques to try to avoid the press at Coleherne. Carolyn would dress as Diana and take off in her friend's red mini in one direction, while her friend headed off in a borrowed car the opposite way. Diana would stage her dates by first meeting at her grandmother's house before leaving in another car to meet the Prince. She escaped out the back door on countless occasions, once even by being lowered down on a set of bedsheets tied together!

This continued throughout the autumn of 1980. It seemed the press and the public just couldn't get enough of this mystery woman who seemed to have captured the heart of a future King. Some have said that the press and the palace pushed Charles into the engagement by making such a fuss over the relationship; and the fact that Diana was a young girl who needed to be treated respectfully. How could he let her down after all the media hype and hysteria over this developing courtship? Her reputation would be ruined.

When there was no engagement announced at Christmas 1980, it's hard to say who was more disappointed – Diana or the waiting public. She had hoped for a ring but was disheartened when she wasn't even invited to Sandringham to spend Christmas with the royal family. This type of invitation was strictly reserved for family members. She moped around Althorp, trying to avoid Raine's probing questions.

In January Charles left for a skiing trip with his friends, but phoned Diana early in February saying he had something to ask her upon his return. Diana thrilled knowing this was "it" and a proposal would be coming soon.

On February 6th, 1981 Diana had her hair and makeup done, and nervously met Charles at Windsor Castle for tea in the nursery. The proposal *did* come but was not the romantic occasion that Diana had imagined. The Prince asked her to marry him, reminded her that she would one day be Queen, and asked her to think about it during her upcoming trip with her mother to Australia. Diana promptly answered "yes" and said that she didn't need to think about it. Then Prince Charles left the room to advise the Queen. It was all over in a matter of just a few minutes. It had been decided to hold the formal engagement announcement upon her return from her trip.

Diana rushed back to the Coleherne flat a short while later, and all the girls looked at her expectantly. "Did he ask?" they cried. Diana said that he had, and she had answered "yes please." The girls all fell giggling on the couch. They piled into a car and drove around Hyde Park talking and laughing together.

Diana and Frances left the next day for a three-week holiday in Australia. Frances and Peter had a large property there, but the two ladies escaped the notice of the paparazzi, and found a secluded beach resort where they talked and planned for a summer wedding. They had managed to elude the press at every turn, and back in London, Fleet Street was awash with rumors that the royal romance was over. Where was Lady Di?

Diana and her mother returned on February 22nd and were whisked through Heathrow by a private security detail. Things had changed for the soon-to-be Princess. She arrived back at the flat to a warm welcome from Carolyn, Virginia and Anne. Flowers from the Prince awaited her as well as a newly-assigned PPO (Personal Protection Officer). He advised that the following morning she would be taken to Clarence House until the engagement on the 24th and from there, she'd be moving to Buckingham Palace until the wedding. He also told her it was her last night of freedom ever for the rest of her life, so she should make the most of it. How prophetic this turned out to be!

It was her final night at Coleherne Court. Although she was to see her friends again (especially Carolyn who remained a lifelong and loyal confidante), she was never to stay again in her single girl flat. The girls piled into Diana's car and circled Hyde Park several times. They talked and talked into the night, and toasted Diana with coca-cola. I'm certain there was lots of hugs, kisses, laughter and tears.

Significant Events that happened at Coleherne Court

- Diana moves to London to live with her mother: 1978
- Diana is invited to her first ball at Buckingham Palace for HRH, Prince Charles' 30th birthday party: 1978
- Diana buys her own flat at Coleherne Court: 1979
- Diana starts to work at Young Kindergarten: 1979
- Diana meets Prince Charles at Petworth House: 1980
- Diana visits Balmoral Castle: 1980
- Prince Charles proposes at Windsor Castle: 1981
- Diana moves out of Coleherne Court: 1981

In Her Own Words

"It was nice being in the flat with the girls. I loved that – it was great. I laughed my head off there. I loved being on my own – a great treat." Diana, Princess of Wales

Coleherne Court Today

This apartment block is still a bank of high-end flats near the Old Brompton Road. Easily accessible by tube, you can see 60 Coleherne Court from the outside only. Nearby Young England Kindergarten is a few tube stops away at Pimlico if you want to see where Diana spent about two years as a Kindergarten Assistant.

FOUR

Clarence House

London, England
(February 1981)

The day before her engagement was announced, Diana moved from Coleherne Court to Clarence House. It was a bittersweet day for the nineteen-year old. She was leaving behind a life and friends that she loved, but trading it all for a new royal life with the Prince of her dreams. She packed up her things and left the girls a jaunty note, "For God's sake, please ring me. I'm going to need it!"

Clarence House had been the first home of Princess Elizabeth and the Duke of Edinburgh when they had married in 1947. It then became the home of Queen

Elizabeth, the Queen Mother until she died in 2002. In 1981, the palace decided it was the best place for Diana to be launched as the new fiancé of the Prince of Wales.

The house was built in the late 1820s by designer John Nash for William, Duke of Clarence. It stands next to St. James Palace in the heart of London, just down the street from Buckingham Palace. It was commissioned by the Duke of Clarence, who later became King William IV. Various other royals lived there, including Queen Victoria's mother, the Duchess of Kent, who was kicked out of Buckingham Palace after her daughter's accession. During World War II, it was used by the Red Cross and St. John Ambulance Brigade as their headquarters. It also suffered bomb damage during the war.

Princess Elizabeth and her new husband, Philip (then known as the Duke and Duchess of Edinburgh) moved into Clarence House in 1949, after a major refurbishment. Prince Charles was born at Buckingham Palace in November 1948. Princess Anne was born at Clarence House in August of 1950. The young family only lived there until 1952 when Elizabeth's father, King George VI unexpectedly died.

The house has four stories, not including attics or basements, and is faced in a pale white stucco with an impressive square design. It has undergone extensive remodeling and reconstruction over the years, most notably after the Second World War, such that relatively little remains of Nash's original structure.

Guests enter via a large porch that leads into the entrance hall. A square garden faces the porch.

It's a large mansion, but still feels like a family home. There are formal rooms such as The Lancaster Room (used as a waiting room for visitors), Morning, Garden and Dining Rooms and Library, and several other sitting and drawing rooms. Much of the antique furniture, rugs, lamps and art pieces have sat unchanged for decades if not generations. The Morning Room still retains the pale gray walls, silk damask curtains and powder blue Chippendale sofas and chairs from the Queen Mother's time. The Dining Room showcases fourteen paintings of Windsor Castle painted by John Piper during World War II at her request. Everywhere the walls and tables are cluttered with pieces of art and framed family photographs which give off a homey feel.

Bedrooms and offices take up space upstairs, and staff rooms are situated at the top of the house. The entire feel of Clarence House is light, spacious and characterful.

For a teenaged girl, it may have seemed a little stuffy and old-fashioned, but certainly familiar in style and decoration to Althorp, or even Park House.

Diana was greeted by a member of staff and was cheered to find a bouquet of flowers from Charles with an accompanying note saying he would join her for dinner that night. It brought up her spirits a bit as she sat in new and strange surroundings. She was surprised to see a note on her pillow from Camilla Parker-Bowles. In it, the older woman congratulated Diana on the engagement and the ring, and invited her to lunch while the Prince was away for three weeks in New Zealand.

"Such exciting news about the engagement. Let's do have lunch when the Prince of Wales goes to Australia and New Zealand. He's going to be away three weeks. I'd love to see the ring. Love, Camilla."

Diana sank onto the bed, the words in the note blurring as her eyes teared up. How had Camilla known she was going to be here at Clarence House when she had just found out herself? The Prince was going to Australia? For three weeks? How had Camilla known this and not Diana? And what about the ring? How could Camilla have known about this and all these things enough in advance to send a note? Diana was in tears again for the second time that day. Why was Charles' friend so informed about her whereabouts and actions? Was the Prince telling Camilla intimate details of their courtship and engagement plans? What the bloody hell was going on?" From Diana, A Spencer in Love.

By now Diana knew that Camilla was a special friend of her fiancé. They had dated in the early 70s before Camilla had married Andrew Parker-Bowles and had two children. She and the Prince had remained friends, and Camilla had consoled the Prince of Wales after the horrible murder of Lord Mountbatten. It's believed that at that time that Charles and Camilla rekindled their physical relationship.

Over the previous few months, Diana had begun to suspect that Camilla was more than a friend. She was always around at weekends no matter where Diana and Charles were invited. She had an unnerving knowledge of Charles' mind. How had Camilla known about Charles' trip when it was news to Diana? And what did she know about the engagement ring that Diana herself did not yet possess? Diana's uneasiness about Camilla's importance in the Prince's life grew.

After dinner at Clarence House with the Prince, Queen Mother and Lady Fermoy, the Garrards royal jeweler arrived with a tray of precious gems to show the future Princess of Wales. She selected the largest blue sapphire, hoping it would become a beautiful ring.

The next morning Diana woke up in a strange suite with no telephone, television or familiar belongings. She had breakfast alone from a tea tray in her room and reviewed the schedule for the day. She would dress and meet the Prince at Buckingham Palace where an official announcement would have already been released to parliament and the press. They were to participate in a short television interview before a photo session in the gardens behind Buckingham Palace. Then a formal dinner with HM, The Queen and Prince Philip. She was also informed that she would no longer be returning to her job at Young England Kindergarten. Although she expected this news, it still gave her a wave of sadness and longing for the children and staff she would not see again.

Diana dressed in the new blue suit and blouse she had bought with her mother just a few days ago. She thought it was smart, and made her feel more grown up. Later she was to look at the newspaper photographs in horror as she judged herself too chubby and dowdy.

The Prince presented her with the finished ring – a large blue sapphire surrounded by diamond; Diana was overwhelmed. Things were moving so fast she could hardly catch her breath.

They were both nervous for the television interview. Charles took the lead, and Diana hoped her smiles and nods were sufficient. At the close, the host asked if the couple were in love. Diana responded immediately with "of course," while Charles glanced at his fiancé and replied, "whatever love is." Although there had been few love words passed between the couple, Diana felt sure Charles would never marry her if he didn't desperately love her as much as she did him. His offhand remark shook her to her core. She smiled weakly, crushed.

The rest of the day passed in a blur. Diana was impressed at the efficiency of the palace machinery as she was whisked from location to location with split second timing. She fell into bed exhausted but thrilled to be officially engaged to the Prince who had been kind and considerate all day.

The next day she was moved to the Buckingham Palace apartments she would occupy until the night before the royal wedding. She would spend her last night as a single woman back at Clarence House before her July 29th wedding. During the intervening five months she would begin her official royal life, prepare for the wedding and try to learn as fast as she possibly could.

Significant Events that happened at Clarence House

- Diana leaves her Coleherne Court flat for a brief stay at Clarence House: 1981
- It is officially announced from Buckingham Palace that His Royal Highness, The Prince of Wales is engaged to Lady Diana Spencer: 1981
- Diana moves to Buckingham Palace until the wedding: 1981

In Her Own Words

"A briefcase comes along on the pretext that Andrew is getting a signet ring for his 21st birthday and along comes these sapphires. I mean nuggets! I suppose I chose it – we all chipped in. The Queen paid for it." Diana, Princess of Wales

Clarence House Today:

As the official London residence of the Prince of Wales, Clarence House is open to visitors on a limited basis each summer – only when the Duke and Duchess of Cornwall are at Balmoral for their summer holiday.

When Charles inherited Clarence House from the Queen Mother in 2002, he redecorated while still keeping the style and ambience of his late grandmother. Charles restored a suite for Camilla, signalling a marriage was most definitely in their future. Besides updating the plumbing, electrical and other needed maintenance, the Prince gave the home a thorough renovation including updating the seven upstairs bedrooms to add ensuite bathrooms. It surprised me to learn there's a cinema in the basement with twenty-one plush red seats!

If you happen to be in London during August, try to make time to visit Clarence House. It's just down the street from Buckingham Palace and is a quick one-hour tour. Only selected state rooms on the first floor are open: Entrance Hall, Lancaster Room, Morning Room, Library, Dining Room, Hall, Horse Corridor and the Garden Room. You'll still get the feel of a royal residence – you can almost see the Queen Mum floating through the rooms.

There are lots of beautiful paintings, and keep a lookout for familiar royals in the many family photos dotting the tables and walls.

Security is very tight, so ensure your tickets are in order and put your camera away – no photos allowed. Check rct.uk/visit/clarence-house for opening times and visitor information.

FIVE

Buckingham Palace

London, England
(1981)

Many people didn't realize that Diana lived at Buckingham Palace during her engagement. She simply disappeared from the streets of London, except when she appeared for official engagements with Prince Charles. She was given a suite of apartments near the old royal nursery.

Buckingham Palace is the official residence and administrative headquarters of the reigning monarch of the United Kingdom. Located in the City of Westminster, the palace is often at the center of state occasions and royal hospitality. It has been a focal point for the British people at times of national rejoicing and mourning. Who doesn't remember the royal family on the balcony in their finery – uniforms, crowns and beautiful gowns – on famous occasions? The famous black and gold gates are a gathering place in good times and bad. When a royal heir is born, an announcement easel is set up just inside the gates. Buckingham Palace is the ultimate symbol of the British monarchy.

Originally known as Buckingham House, the core of today's palace was a large townhouse built for the Duke of Buckingham in 1703. King George III bought it in 1761 and it has been enlarged upon and improved since then. Queen Victoria was the first monarch to use it as the official London residence of the reigning sovereign, and it's been used for that purpose ever since.

The palace chapel was destroyed by a German bomb during World War II, one of nine palace bombings between 1939 and 1945. Two bombs landed just feet away from King George VI and Queen Elizabeth as they sat in their drawing room. Luckily, they weren't injured, but the Queen famously said "Now we can look the East End in the face." This was a tribute to the thousands of homeless residents who were bombed nightly during the war. It endeared her and the King to the British people.

There are 775 rooms, including 19 state rooms, 52 principal bedrooms, 188 staff bedrooms, 92 offices, and 78 bathrooms. The palace also has its own post office, cinema, swimming pool, doctor's surgery, and jeweler's workshop. More than 50,000 people visit the Palace each year as guests to State banquets, lunches, dinners, receptions and Garden Parties. Her Majesty also holds weekly audiences with the Prime Minister and receives newly-appointed foreign Ambassadors at Buckingham Palace.

Famous principal (or state) rooms include the Music Room, Blue and the White Drawing Rooms, Picture

Gallery, Throne Room and Green Drawing Room. The Green Drawing Room serves as a huge anteroom to the Throne Room and is part of the ceremonial route to the throne from the Guard Room at the top of the Grand Staircase. The Throne Room is commonly used now for formal family portraits after royal weddings.

Many famous people have met the Queen after climbing the Grand Staircase – American presidents, world leaders, artists, musicians and many notable visitors. At State visits, these important guests are treated to elaborate dinners in the formal Ballroom – the largest room in the house. The smaller State Dining Room is used for more informal charity dinners. The long Picture Gallery and White Drawing room with its elaborate chandelier are used to host receptions for groups of 300 or so. The White Drawing Room boasts a concealed door to the left of the fireplace for discreet getaways when the Queen needs a quick escape!

The Palace houses countless pieces of priceless art as part of The Royal Collection including paintings, sculpture, furniture, clocks and porcelain. Many of these art objects date back hundreds of years through prior monarchs like Queen Victoria and King George III. Imagine owning original Rembrandt paintings or a Queen Victoria piano!

Directly underneath the State Apartments are the slightly less formal semi-state apartments. Opening from the Marble Hall, these rooms are used for more casual entertaining, such as luncheon parties and private audiences. At the center of this suite is the Bow Room, through which tens of thousands of guests pass annually to the Queen's Garden Parties in the gardens. The Queen and Prince Philip use a smaller suite of private rooms in the north wing. The offices of those who support the day-to-day activities and duties of The Queen such as the

Private Secretary's Office and the Privy Purse and Treasurer's Office are also located at Buckingham Palace.

Buckingham Palace is the official site for investitures, state banquets, and other public and private ceremonial occasions.

The largest private garden in London is located at the rear of the palace. It is here that the Queen hosts her annual garden parties each summer, and holds large functions to celebrate royal milestones, such as jubilees. It covers forty acres and includes a helicopter landing area, a lake, and a private tennis court.

All the royal carriages including the Gold State Coach are housed at the Royal Mews, right next door to the palace. The famous ceremonial approach route to the palace is called The Mall and, was designed by Sir Aston Webb and completed in 1911 as part of a grand memorial to Queen Victoria. It extends from Admiralty Arch, across St. James's Park to the Victoria Memorial. This route is used by the cavalcades and motorcades of visiting heads of state, and by the royal family on state occasions such as royal weddings and the annual celebration of the Queen's birthday called Trooping the Colour.

The Forecourt of Buckingham Palace is used for the Changing of the Guard, a major daily ceremony and tourist attraction.

For such a large estate, Buckingham Palace was surprisingly empty and somewhat desolate. Many of the 600 rooms were only used for special ceremonies and occasions. Each of the palace's inhabitants had their own set of private apartments and didn't see or interact with each other on a daily basis. Diana was shocked to learn that Charles sent a note via a household of footmen in order to meet with his own parents. The family did not dine together or otherwise spend any time in each other's company. Diana hadn't fooled herself into thinking it was a happy family all the time, but she hadn't expected this utter isolation either.

Although her suite of rooms was on the same floor as Prince Charles, it seemed as if they were still miles apart. The Prince left early each day for local or out-of-town engagements. He was only able to dine with Diana once or twice a week. A three-week trip to Australia and New Zealand, which had been planned long before their engagement, was looming and Diana dreaded the thought of being without her new fiancé for weeks. He truly seemed disappointed to have to leave Diana to cope on her own, but the royal diary might as well have been set in stone. Diana would have loved to join Charles on the trip, but it had not been planned; and, in any case, she had wedding activities to keep her busy. As the date for his departure neared, she couldn't help clutching to him and their time together with a sense of desperation. From Diana, A Spencer in Love.

Diana moved into Buckingham Palace shortly after her engagement to Prince Charles was formally announced. She moved into a suite of rooms which included a bedroom, small sitting room and bathroom. Diana was assigned a lady's maid, and two palace officials were on hand to help her understand her new role.

This was a lonely time for nineteen-year old Diana. Prince Charles had left for a long-planned overseas visit to New Zealand, and she was left virtually on her own in the palace. The royal family does not meet for nightly dinners, nor spend time casually together on a day-to-day basis. They all have busy and separate schedules of charity events, meetings and other commitments. Diana occasionally dropped by to say hello to the Queen after her daily swim in the Buckingham Palace pool, but largely kept to herself throughout these lonely months.

Diana decided she needed to adapt to this new life on her own, and barely saw her old friends from Coleherne Court. Perhaps she was ashamed at how boring and stifling her new life was. When she did see her friends, they were shocked at how thin she had become, and that she seemed to be constantly in tears. It's believed that Diana's bulimia dates to this time, when Charles told she was getting chubby after the engagement was announced.

Diana's main activities during the five months before wedding included choosing and getting fitted for a complete royal wardrobe, and preparing for the biggest royal wedding ever to be held in the United Kingdom. She did get some help from her mother with the shopping and planning, but Frances was a hands-off Mom who wanted to let her daughter make their own decisions.

Diana loved designing her own wedding gown with the help of David and Elizabeth Emmanuel – two young British designers. She was a bit surprised that she had been given a free hand to choose the gown she wanted, but she decided to indulge her inner princess and go over the top with the dress. She loved bows, lace and ruffles, and the dress had plenty of all of them. She had heard that the longest royal train had been 20 feet long, so she wanted to top this with a 25-foot-long train. She would, of course, wear the Spencer tiara and other priceless gems. As the months went by, the dress had to be taken in again and again as Diana lost more and more weight. Eventually, she lost somewhere around twenty pounds in this short five-month period. Whether it was unrelenting press scrutiny, wedding jitters, trying to get accustomed to royal life or insecurity about her future husband and Camilla, Diana was under enormous stress at this time, and remember – she was only nineteen years old with almost no one to guide her.

It's been falsely reported that the Queen Mum took Diana under her wing and helped acclimatize her to royal life. This is completely untrue. None of the senior royals would ever be expected to train or guide new family members – this would be unheard-of and disrespectful to their status. Diana was from an old, distinguished and aristocratic British family (some say more English than the royals themselves), and she was expected to simply fit into the new regime.

Diana *did* receive assistance from the Queen's lady-in-waiting Lady Susan Hussey and Prince Charles' Assistant Private Secretary Oliver Everett. They briefed her on protocol, how to smile, wave, curtsey and address dignitaries correctly, and a myriad of other rules of being royal. They also gave her history books to read and absorb. She took driving lessons, was schooled in security measures, and advised about the annual requirements in the royal diary. It was overwhelming and exhausting for a young girl. Not to mention boring – especially the book learning which was challenging for someone with no "O" levels in her academic background.

Adding to her frustration was the absence of her new fiancé to help and support her. When they dated, Diana and Charles seemed to always be surrounded by the Prince's friends and courtiers. The number of times that they had been alone together could practically be counted on one hand. But once they were engaged, Diana expected this all to change. Of course, Charles would spend much more time with her!

But this was not to be. At the age of thirty-two, the Prince of Wales had an extremely busy diary of local and overseas royal and charitable engagements, numerous and varied all-consuming hobbies, and a large circle of friends. The royal diary is set six months in advance, so the Prince was committed to a full slate of duties and obligations long before he was engaged. These could not be altered – even should Charles wish to do so – and this was not even a matter for consideration.

Charles empathized with his confused and forlorn fiancé, but felt somewhat helpless. He provided as much support as he could, given his commitments and priorities. He had a difficult time understanding this skittish and emotional girl, but put it down to wedding nerves and her tender age.

The wedding of the century took place on Wednesday, July 29, 1981. The bride was barely twenty years old and the storybook fairy tale princess that the world had waited for. The groom was a dashing military prince and future King of England. As the Archbishop of Canterbury said: "This is the stuff of which fairy tales are made."

The couple honeymooned aboard the royal yacht Britannia, and at the Balmoral Estate in Scotland. Diana continued to lose weight and was a nervous and jumpy newlywed.

Significant Events that happened at Buckingham Palace

- Diana moves into Buckingham Palace until her wedding: 1981
- Wedding of HRH, Prince Charles and Lady Diana Spencer: 1981

In Her Own Words

"I don't know what to do. I feel so unhappy here. Charles doesn't understand me. He would prefer to be out shooting or stalking or riding or chatting with mother than be with me. Can't he understand that I need him to look after me? I feel he's abandoned me. He just leaves me here all day. I hate it." Diana, Princess of Wales.

SIX

The Royal Yacht Britannia

Mediterranean Cruise
(1981)

Diana and Charles spent the first part of their honeymoon aboard The Royal Yacht Britannia. After a short two-day stay after the wedding at Broadlands (the family home of the Prince's great-uncle Mountbatten), the newlyweds boarded Britannia From Gibraltar, Spain and cruised the Mediterranean and Greek Islands for two weeks.

This was Diana's second time aboard the ship, having spent a weekend aboard Britannia early in the courtship during Cowes week. I'm sure both she and Charles were exhausted from the wedding and intense press scrutiny, and were looking forward to a relaxing time to really get to know each other on their own.

HMS Britannia was built for Her Majesty the Queen by John Brown & Co. in 1952, shortly after the death of her father. The Queen and Prince Philip had a large say in the design and outfitting of the ship and the Queen paid great attention to detail – as she does in all things. The name was a closely guarded secret until its launch on April 16, 1953 when Her Majesty made this announcement, "I name this ship Britannia. I wish success to her and all those who sail in her."

Britannia was the last of 83 royal ships to be commissioned. *The Victoria and Albert III* had served four sovereigns before being de-commissioned in 1939.

The outfitting of Britannia reflected the austerity of post-war England. When I visited the ship, I was a little surprised at the small size and modest appointments of the royal apartments. It's understandable that a ship is much smaller than a royal palace, but the Queen deliberately chose understated elegance.

The State Drawing Room was used for family gatherings and was the main entertaining space for on-board visitors. It's spacious with light furniture and carpets. A Welmar grand piano was bolted to the floor in case of heavy weather. Noel Coward and Princess Diana both played it, and Princess Margaret led singalongs around it. The family also played card games and charades in this comfy room.

The State Dining Room was the grandest room onboard and the Queen hosted many famous guests here including Winston Churchill, Bill Clinton and Nelson Mandela. Setting the table for a formal dinner onboard Britannia was as meticulous as any state dinner at Buckingham Palace. It would have taken three hours to set the table for

50+ guests including exacting measurements between the positions of cutlery and dishes. The room also did double duty as a cinema, church and even dance floor.

The Queen's and Duke's separate Sitting Rooms were decorated to their individual tastes – the Duke's being much more masculine. A miniature model of the *HMS Magpie* – Philip's first naval command – took pride of place over the desk. The Queen and the Duke had separate bedrooms, with an adjoining door between.

Prince Charles and Princess Diana had their own suite across the passageway from the older generation. A double bed was installed for the honeymooners (replacing the existing single beds) but it's still a small room. They had dressing and sitting rooms that led to a private veranda.

The Prince and Princess of Wales' Bedroom Suite

A sun lounge opened up to the main deck where the royal family spent time in good weather.

Below deck Britannia was a working ship. There were twenty-one officers and 220 Royal Yachtsman as the primary crew. They communicated via hand signals and wore soft-soled shoes to ensure the royal family were never disturbed. The same high standards expected at any royal palace were also demanded aboard Britannia. A Buckingham Palace chef cooked meals for the Queen and royal family in a separate galley from the officers and other crew.

Queen Elizabeth loved Britannia and enjoyed many family and state voyages. She felt at her most relaxed on her private yacht, and eagerly anticipated the annual family vacations. The royal children loved the summer holiday cruises aboard the secluded environment with treasure hunts, shore picnic lunches and water fights put on by the ship's company. Visits to the Queen Mother at her Scottish Castle of Mey enroute to Balmoral were eagerly anticipated by all.

My 2019 visit to the Royal Yacht Britannia

When the newly-married Prince and Princess of Wales boarded Britannia in August of 1981, they were sorely in need of rest, relaxation and alone time.

Diana had been continuously losing weight through the six-month engagement, fighting her insecurities and fears through the eating disorder bulimia. The disease is characterized by bouts of binge eating, followed by self-induced vomiting. The *high* of eating is overshadowed by the *low* and self-loathing that accompanies the purging. It's a vicious cycle that is incredibly damaging to self-esteem.

Diana had thought the honeymoon would be a magical time of intimacy and bonding with her dashing new husband.

However, the Prince had different ideas of what constituted a wonderful honeymoon experience. Along with his painting gear, he had brought along seven books by his mentor Laurens Van Der Post, a South African soldier, adventurer, philosopher and writer. Charles envisioned sunning on deck with his wife, discussing some of the philosophies of Van Der Post. The idea appalled his young wife who hid her romance novels from her new husband.

They had changed for lunch, and Charles lovingly presented the books.

"Diana, we're going to have a splendid time with these books. I've brought along enough for us to share. We can each read them and discuss meaningful passages at mealtimes or whilst sunning on the deck." Charles was delighted with his own idea.

Diana's heart sunk to her toes. Didn't Charles know she couldn't manage that heavy reading? She couldn't even cope with staff briefs, let alone wade through the massive and complex psychological theories. This was a honeymoon???"
From Diana, A Spencer in Love

Diana's idea of an ideal honeymoon was fun in the sun, swimming and windsurfing, followed by plenty of private time with her new husband. At least they had one thing in common – they were both sun lovers. The newlyweds enjoyed the outdoors together – swimming, snorkeling and sunbathing.

However, Diana's bulimia overshadowed it all. Her suspicions that Charles was still involved with his ex-mistress continued to grow. He still spoke to Camilla every day on the phone – although he probably tried to hide this from his new wife. Being in such close quarters with his bride couldn't hide Diana's rampant bouts of binging and purging. The two ate all their meals together, and Diana would often excuse herself to the bathroom. The staff were amazed at how much the Princess would eat, and yet visibly grew thinner over the two-week cruise. Both Charles and Diana loved ice cream and ate it almost every meal. Sadly, Diana rarely kept it down. Charles would have been bewildered and probably repulsed by a disease he couldn't comprehend.

It didn't help the intimacy level to have hundreds of crewmen onboard, quiet as they were. Diana joked with many of them in her casual way, but still felt isolated. I imagine she often frequented the below-deck NAAFI (Navy, Army and Air Force Institute) shop for sweets, home-made fudge and a jokey chat with young sailors.

The young couple ate with the captain and senior officers most nights in the formal State Dining Room. They took a tender ashore on a few occasions for beach picnics and barbecues, but had to be mindful of security issues and lurking paparazzi. Even on a luxurious yacht, there must have been moments of claustrophobia. Diana had no contact with family and friends as the royals sailed through the Mediterranean.

The two did have some loving moments together, holding hands and chatting together over quiet lunches in their private sitting room. In the evenings they watched movies including the wedding video, and listened to music together. By the end of the two weeks, crew members commented they "couldn't keep their hands off each other" so there was certainly some love and romance between the newly wedded couple. And amazingly enough, the press corps never found or disturbed them, despite their best efforts. This must have been a huge relief.

There were two serious blow-ups between the Prince and Princess aboard Britannia – both over Camilla Parker-Bowles. The first occurred when the couple were reviewing their diaries and photos of Camilla fell out of Charles' book. A "filthy row" ensued as Diana accused her husband of an ongoing affair with the married woman, while he calmly defended their platonic relationship.

The second argument erupted at the end of the trip – shortly before docking and embarking on the second part of the honeymoon at Balmoral Castle. While dressing for a formal dinner with the Egyptian President Muhammad Anwar el-Sadat and his wife Jehan, Charles donned a pair of gold cufflinks in the shape of intertwining "Cs." Diana pounced and asked Charles if Camilla had given him these custom-made jewelry pieces. He calmly confirmed that Camilla had given him the gift of the cufflinks in simple friendship. Diana demanded that he change them and Charles refused. Another volatile argument ensued with a pattern that was to repeat many times in the marriage: Diana accusing and screaming while Charles became distant and remote. It was not a healthy way to argue.

Diana was teary-eyed and quiet at the official dinner, which was awkward for hosts and guests alike.

On the final night, the crew and staff presented a theatrical entertainment for the royal couple. A costumed song and dance were performed, and a sailor dressed in woman's clothing impersonated the Princess telling salty jokes. It was a casual and fun evening.

The next morning, August 16th, the crew lined the deck, saluted and gave three cheers to the departing couple. They were then driven to Hurghada to board a train for the next leg of their honeymoon – Balmoral Castle in Scotland. From what we know now, Diana was probably filled with immense dread about the coming weeks.

Significant Events that happened aboard The Royal Yacht Britannia

- Diana and Charles spend the first two weeks of their honeymoon aboard the yacht: 1981
- Diana and Charles vacation aboard the ship prior to the annual Balmoral holiday: intermittently 1982 – 1992
- Diana and Charles travel to Canada for an official visit – Diana is famously photographed reuniting with her sons aboard the ship: 1991

In Her Own Words

"We had to entertain in the boardroom on Britannia, which were all the top people every night so there was never any time on our own. Found this very difficult to accept. By then the bulimia was appalling, absolutely appalling." Diana, Princess of Wales.

The Royal Yacht Britannia Today:

In June 1994, John Major's Government announced there would be no refit for HMY Britannia as the costs would be too great. After a long and successful career spanning 44 years and travelling over a million miles around the globe, it was announced that the last Royal Yacht was to be decommissioned.

There was no immediate decision about a replacement, but the question of a new Royal Yacht became a political issue in the run up to the 1997 General Election. After the election, the new Labor Government eventually confirmed in October 1997 there would be no replacement for Britannia. The Queen sadly agreed.

Britannia was de-commissioned on December 11, 1997 at Portsmouth after a final voyage around the U.K., calling at six ports. The Queen was piped off the ship at 3:01 p.m. and all the clocks aboard Britannia are permanently set at this time.

This was a difficult decision for the Queen. She loved Britannia and had spent countless happy hours aboard the ship with her family and friends. She was not the only one to shed a tear at the decommissioning ceremony, but it was certainly an emotional moment for the monarch.

"It is with sadness that we must now say goodbye to BRITANNIA. It is appropriate that with this final event she bows out in the style which is so typical of the manner in which her business has always been conducted." Elizabeth R and Philip, 11th December 1997.

The decommissioned yacht is permanently docked in the Port of Leith in Edinburgh, Scotland. It's been open to the public since 1998 and attracts 300,000 visitors annually.

It's well worth a half-day visit. It's about a half-hour taxi ride from the center of Edinburgh. You can access the ship via the Ocean Terminal Shopping Centre (follow the signs) and the self-guided audio tour will walk you through the entire ship. Five decks are open for viewing including the Main Deck, Royal Apartments, State Dining Room, Engine Room,

Yachtsmen's Quarters and so much more!

I thoroughly enjoyed my visit in 2019. You can really feel the spirit of the royals when you're on board. Peek into The Sun Lounge which was The Queen's favorite room for breakfast and afternoon tea, stand on the Verandah Deck and gaze out to sea, look into Charles and Diana's honeymoon suite, and picture yourself sitting at the table set in the Dining Room. Imagine greeting world leaders in the State Dining Room and Anteroom. Enjoy all the historic paintings, pictures and artifacts displayed throughout the ship, and picture yourself being invited into the State Drawing Room for a formal reception with the royal family.

Tour the lower decks to see the sailors and officers' quarters & dining rooms, engine room and all the service areas needed to support what is essentially a royal palace on water. It's a comprehensive and moving experience to be this close to royal life.

BONUS: Unlike most royal residences, you are allowed to take photos and videos onboard so snap away.

You can also enjoy tea and cakes at the Royal Deck Tea Room, and visit the gift shop for souvenirs.

Visit <u>royalyachtbritannia.co.uk</u> for opening times and visitor information.

SEVEN

Balmoral Castle

Ballater, Scotland
(1981 & ongoing)

When Diana visited Balmoral Castle during her honeymoon, this wasn't her first holiday at the family retreat. She had been to the Scottish ancestral home of the royals the previous summer and had passed the "Balmoral Test" and demonstrated "Balmorality" – the crucial ability to fit in with the royal family at their most relaxed, doing what they do best – hunting, fishing, hiking and enjoying the Scottish countryside.

Diana had been invited by the Queen herself during the summer of 1980 to spend a weekend at Balmoral. The invitation itself was an incredible statement of support for the budding royal romance.

In fact, Charles and Diana's relationship had been discovered at Balmoral. Photographers with long lens spied a girl sitting on a riverbank while Charles fished nearby. Diana spotted them and quickly ran up the hill, hid behind a tree, and took out her compact mirror to spy on the invaders. She was also seen at Aberdeen airport, and clever paparazzi put two and two together and got Lady Diana Spencer.

Diana showed a great interest in the outdoor life, spending hours watching Charles fish the River Dee, hunting, walking for miles and helping out with the washing up at the frequent barbecues and picnics. The only activity that Diana shied away from was horseback riding. She had fallen off a horse as a child, and had a lingering fear of horses. Nonetheless, the Queen and Duke were delighted with Diana and how relaxed and comfortable she was hiking across the moors in the morning and dressing up in evening wear and jewels for a formal dinner in the Ballroom at night.

Prince Charles met Diana later that afternoon for another walk. It was drizzling but Diana borrowed a mac from a hook at the cottage. She wouldn't have dreamed of refusing the Prince on account of the weather. As with the day before, the Prince set a brisk pace as they roamed over the wet moors. After seeing the demands on the Prince's time in social settings, Diana was thrilled to have him all to herself. He had greeted her warmly and tucked her arm under his. She felt quite protected and safe.

Today the Prince seemed eager to talk about his new purchase – a country home called Highgrove House in the Cotswolds. Diana paid rapt attention as they tromped through the rain.

"I've been on the lookout for a country home for some time now, Diana," he started. "One needs a place of retreat, a place to get away from the rigors of duties and appointments. I can't get away to my beloved Balmoral every weekend, more's the pity." He stopped and pointed his walking stick to the expansive fields surrounding them. From Diana, A Spencer in Love.

Some of Diana's critics have claimed that Diana faked her interest and appreciation for Balmoral and its lifestyle. She was truly a city girl at heart and even though she had grown up on country estates, she didn't really enjoy long hikes, fishing or hunting. She was also uncomfortable with the unflinching royal schedule that was strictly adhered to every summer – the multiple wardrobe changes per day, close quarters with all the royal family and their guests, and the constant conversation of horses and dogs. She found it all suffocating and would seek any opportunity to avoid spending time there. If she was on her best behaviour to impress Charles and his mother that first summer we'll never know for sure, but it seems likely she did what many young girls have done for centuries – feign an interest in their boyfriend's hobbies and passions during the courtship phase. And then hope to change them once married. A deadly expectation!

Balmoral is one of only two privately-owned royal residences. The other is Sandringham in Norfolk, England.

Balmoral was leased by Queen Victoria and Prince Albert in 1848, after them both having fallen in love with Scotland and the Highlands. It reminded them both of landscapes in Germany, Albert's homeland, and promised an ideal holiday estate. By 1862, Victoria and Albert completed negotiations to purchase Balmoral outright.

The original house was deemed too small for their needs, and Prince Albert energetically assumed the lead role in designing the new castle. The architect was William Smith of local Aberdeen who built the new castle from local white granite. It consisted of two main blocks, each arranged around a courtyard. The southwestern block contains the main rooms, while the northeastern contains the service wings. At the southeast is an 80-foot tall clock tower topped with turrets. The new premises were built 100 yards away from the old estate which the family occupied during the intervening years. The royals took possession in 1855 and the Queen called it "my dear paradise in the Highlands." The rounded columns and turrets are reminiscent of castles such as might be found in Grimm's German fairy tales – certainly a nod to Albert's background.

The estate comprises an area of approximately 50,000 acres. It is a working property, including grouse moors, forestry, and farmland, as well as managed herds of deer, cattle and ponies. There are vast gardens that provide all the organic vegetables and flowers for the royal family during their annual two-month stay. Balmoral is located near the village of Crathie, about 10 km west of Ballater in Aberdeenshire, Scotland. The closest airport is Aberdeen and it's an hour's drive from there to the remote castle. An eight-hour drive from London, the short 90-minute flight makes it easy for the royals to escape to their beloved Scottish retreat.

The River Dee runs through the property and is a favorite spot for fishing and picnicking. There are seven large hills within the estate, the highest being Lochnager at 3,789 feet which was the setting for a children's story, *The Old Man of Lochnagar*, written by Prince Charles in 1980.

Balmoral is the hub of the community, with over 150 properties on site and is self-sustaining in terms of maintenance and support, providing many jobs for locals. Provisions and groceries are obtained in nearby Ballater, and the royals attend the local Crathie church each Sunday.

It can be quite cold in Northern Scotland, and Balmoral is known to be chilly and drafty. The interior is covered with tartan in virtually every room: carpets, wall coverings, pillows and tablecloths. There are dozens of stag heads displayed on the walls – particularly in the Ballroom where they are lined across the tops of the walls. Paintings of hunting and stalking dot the hallways. The royals themselves embrace Scottish habits when staying at their summer home, sporting kilts and tartan skirts on a daily basis.

Since Victoria and Albert moved into the spacious estate, four British monarchs and their families have embraced Balmoral life: King Edward VII, King George V and VI, and our current Queen Elizabeth II. It's always been a treasured family holiday oasis.

They entered the drawing room at Balmoral shortly before half-past seven. It was a sight that Diana would never forget. Prince Charles and the young Princes Andrew and Edward were resplendent in Scottish highland tartan kilts. The Queen Mother sat in an armchair with Diana's grandmother Lady Fermoy attending her. She was as diminutive as Diana had thought from pictures, but wasn't quite so friendly. She carried more of a disapproving look than the smiling geniality seen in public. Princess Margaret sat on a long sofa in a royal blue dress, smoking a cigarette as she chatted with some unknown guests. Diana recognized some familiar faces from the Britannia trip – the P-T's, Soames' and the ever-present Camilla Parker-Bowles – although Camilla's husband Andrew was not in sight. The room sparkled with ladies' gowns and jewels, and the men swaggered about in tartan kilts.

Prince Charles greeted Diana and her family with a kiss, and made introductions all around. Diana smiled and shook hands with everyone, and then kissed her grandmother.

Prince Andrew bounded to Diana's side and greeted her with an exuberant hug. He was a handsome, dark-haired twenty-year old version of his older brother. "Don't sit there Diana," he whispered, pointing to an embroidered wingchair. "That's Queen Victoria's chair, and no one is allowed to sit in it." From Diana, A Spencer in Love.

It's hard to know if Diana was dreading or looking forward to the Balmoral portion of her honeymoon. On some level she must have been anticipating finally having her husband to herself for an extended period. They stayed from August to September in that late summer and fall of 1981 – quite a prolonged period of time.

However, it must be difficult to be on honeymoon with your in-laws, extended family and a parade of important visitors including Prime Ministers and foreign dignitaries. Especially the most royal family in the world!

We've all seen the photo call with a beaming newlywed couple in Highland tweeds by the River Dee, extolling the virtues of married life. But behind those smiles was a relationship already in trouble. Diana was obsessed with Charles' ongoing friendship with Camilla Parker-Bowles, and this made her insecure and jealous. Her bulimia was raging which led to drastic mood swings and emotional outbursts.

To be fair, Prince Charles was incredibly worried about his young bride. He had waited years to find the right wife that could handle the royal pressures, and Diana was struggling to cope right from the beginning. The happy-go-lucky friendly, funny, sociable young bride had turned into a fragile, accusatory and reclusive wife. He simply didn't know how to deal with her eating disorder, its symptoms or the emotions it brought out in Diana.

Charles slipped into Balmoral life with the ease of sliding into a pair of comfortable slippers. Spending hours each day hiking, sitting on a mountain top, reading deeply spiritual books, solitary painting, fishing and hunting were his respite from an incredibly busy and stressful life. Rain or shine. And it rains a lot in Scotland.

Diana didn't care for any of these activities and so was bored and restless. In a desperate effort to cheer her up, Charles invited her old flat mate and friend Carolyn Pride for a weekend.

And still the Princess got thinner and thinner. Diana found the stresses of living with the royal family in such close quarters stifling, and with Charles gone for hours each day in his individual pursuits, she was also lonely.

To help his distressed wife, Charles moved them into Craigowan Lodge on the estate for some urgently-needed privacy. Diana then spent her days with her tapestry projects as Charles joined the day-long stag-hunting parties. There surely must have been some fun and intimate times between the couple, but none have been officially reported.

In a critical attempt to help his wife, Charles arranged a trip to London for her to speak to a number of doctors and psychologists. Diana later claimed she resisted this urge to "fix her" and rejected the Valium prescriptions. She also kept her eating disorder a secret from the physicians, so this well-meaning effort by her husband was doomed to fail.

She attended her first Braemar Gathering in September, a local tradition of Scottish competitions and celebrations. She joined the annual Ghillies Ball – a dance where staff and royals dance together in Balmoral's Ballroom in full kilts and royal regalia. She probably enjoyed these social occasions where she could talk to some of the locals in a more relaxed setting. The Ghillies Ball has been held each year since Victorian times and Diana would have attended at least ten of them over her marriage with the Prince of Wales.

By October, Diana was longing to return to London and take up official duties. She was thrilled to discover she was pregnant, and everyone believed that the charming, adaptable and fresh-faced young Diana would soon return. But that girl was gone forever.

Significant Events that happened at Balmoral Castle

- The Queen invites Diana for a Balmoral weekend: 1980
- Diana and Charles honeymoon at the Castle: 1981
- Braemar Gatherings and Ghillies Balls: annually
- The royal family hears of Princess Diana's death: 1997

In Her Own Words

"I don't know what to do here, I feel so unhappy here. Charles doesn't understand me. He would prefer to be out shooting or stalking or riding or chatting with his mother rather than be with me. Can't he understand that I need him to look after me? I feel he's abandoned me. He just leaves me here all day. I hate it."
Diana, Princess of Wales.

Balmoral 2019

Balmoral Castle Today:

Balmoral is still the summer retreat for the Queen and the rest of the royal family. Her Majesty and Duke of Edinburgh vacation there from early August till October. The rest of the family come for shorter visits to accommodate their own busy schedules. The Queen still conducts her daily business all summer from the Castle, handling her red boxes and inviting Prime Ministers and their families for holidays.

Happily, Balmoral is open to the public from approximately April till the Queen arrives in August. There are also some winter events.

You will definitely have to plan your visit because the castle is in a remote area in Northern Scotland. Balmoral is an hour's drive from Aberdeen airport and you can rent a car if you are brave. Or take a taxi or bus from nearby Ballater. It's approximately an eight-hour drive from London. Train service will get you there as well, but be prepared for an overnight trip with connecting trains.

You'll enter the Castle via a bridge over the River Dee. After a short walk or cart ride, you can purchase an audio tour and walk the estate. There is a cafe and gift shop to enhance your visit.

As the castle is a private home, the only room that is open to the public is the Ballroom, so be sure to spend as much time soaking in the environment as you can. As you gaze towards the balcony with two staircases opening on either side, picture the Queen and rest of the royal family appearing in their evening wear, tartans, tiaras and other finery to host a Ghillies Ball or special event. You can almost see Diana descending on Prince Charles' arm before the Queen and Duke make their entrance.

The vast gardens are available to tour and they are wonderful. All of the vegetable and fruit crops are designed to be in season when the Queen is in residence. The flowers are spectacular, including the water garden. You can see some of the outbuildings like the Garden Cottage and Hunting Shed. You're free to take photos outside but not in the Ballroom.

The Duke and Duchess of Rothesay (as Charles and Camilla are known in Scotland) stay at nearby Birkhall when they holiday at Balmoral but this is not open to visitors. You can tour local Ballater which is a lovely town. Keep an eye out for royal warrants over the shop signs that have been honored with the Queen's patronage. Many people visit the area for the hiking, fishing and golf, not to mention the local whiskey.

I loved Balmoral and hope to visit again in the future. Although not much of the Castle is open to visitors, the entire Scottish experience is fascinating and rewarding. The people are warm, friendly and helpful. Neil at Coyle's B&B in Ballater was an extraordinary host, driving to pick me up when I had a car breakdown. He even taxied me to Balmoral the next day.

Edinburgh is about a three-hour drive south from Balmoral and also worth a visit. You can tour Britannia, Holyrood House which is the Queen's official residence in Scotland; and Edinburgh Castle. Outlander fans can also seek out day tours to get a glimpse of the 1700's life of Jamie and Claire Fraser.

Visit balmoralcastle.com for opening times and visitor information.

EIGHT

Buckingham Palace

London, England
(1981 – 1982)

After their honeymoon, the new Princess of Wales moved into the Prince's apartments at Buckingham Palace. Diana longed for her own home, and she was about to have two of them – but just not yet.

Charles had his suite of rooms redecorated as a young man, including office, sitting room, blue bedroom and private bathroom. There were lots of books and objects collected from his travels. His bedroom held a wide four-poster bed with the customary emergency call button nearby. The overall effect was masculine and probably not

71

to a young wife's taste – especially the royal cartoons lining the bathroom walls.

The Prince had purchased a country home – Highgrove House – in Gloucestershire. He had taken Diana to see it during their courtship and had asked for her help in decorating and refurbishing it. Diana had enlisted the help of her mother Frances and her designer, Dudlay Poplak to usher in light and bright colors to the manor house.

At the same time, the Queen had given the couple Apartments 8 and 9 of Kensington Palace which would become their London base. Diana was delighted about this development, but also dismayed at the delays in setting up house until this residence was remodeled and brought up-to-date. Diana was also overseeing this project and given the couple's extended three-month honeymoon, further delays had been inevitable. Now it looked like it would still be months before they could move into either home. Diana consoled herself that it would be well worth it in the end but living in Charles' bachelor suite in the austere Buckingham Palace was difficult.

Three months after the wedding, Diana discovered she was pregnant. She was absolutely thrilled and proud to be fulfilling her role to provide an heir to the throne. Charles perhaps was not as enthusiastic. He had hoped to wait until the two of them had settled more into the marriage – perhaps waiting a year or two. Diana knew that having a baby early would be the best thing for the marriage and the royal family. Charles quickly warmed to the idea of welcoming a Prince or Princess to the royal nursery.

Unfortunately, Diana was struck with crushing morning sickness for much of her pregnancy. This made it even more difficult to carry out her extensive new duties, especially while the public remained unaware of her condition.

The press and paparazzi interest in the Princess of Wales had only intensified since the wedding. They simply could not get enough of the lovely Princess. On royal walkabouts the crowds shouted for her endlessly. She smiled, waved and accepted countless bouquets of flowers. She loved meeting the people – especially the very old and very young.

The royal couple's first visit to Wales was a smashing success. The crowds went wild for the Princess, and she endeared herself even further by staying outside to greet them in the pouring rain. When her pregnancy was announced shortly afterwards, the public love affair with the Princess of Wales rose to new heights. Any thoughts or hopes that media attention would settle down were gone forever.

"It's rather hard to explain to someone who doesn't live it, isn't it, Sarah?" Diana turned to her pal from the palace for support. "People come and go so often, staff changes overnight it seems, you almost feel adrift in a sea – but yet never alone. It's quite a strange feeling. You want to get close to people – especially those around you every day like PPOs, butlers, dressers and chauffeurs. But if you do, they can turn on you, write books about you, go to the press. It's extremely difficult to know who to trust. So for me, I just go with my instinct. It's the only way to manage at all. From Diana, A Spencer in Turmoil

Diana settled in to her new life as the Princess of Wales with a reduced schedule due to her pregnancy. She enjoyed all the rituals of her first Christmas at Sandringham with the whole royal family. I'm sure it must have been bittersweet being in the "big house" next to her childhood Park House home.

As her pregnancy advanced, she stayed home more while the Prince continued his vigorous round of royal duties and played polo as much as the schedule allowed. Diana's last official engagement was Trooping the Color –

the official celebration of the Queen's birthday on June 12th. Standing on the balcony for the first time since her wedding almost twelve months before, Diana would have certainly been lost in memories of how far she had come in just less than a year.

On June 21st, 1982 after a sixteen-hour labor, Diana delivered a healthy 7 ½ pound baby boy. William Arthur Philip Louis Wales was the first heir to the throne to be born in a hospital instead of at home. When Charles and Diana appeared at the door of the Lindo Wing of St. Mary's Hospital the following day, the crowds and world went crazy for this tiny Prince in this perfect family. Both Diana and Charles were ecstatic with their new son. All they needed now was a home of their own.

Significant Events that happened at Buckingham Palace

- Announcement of the pregnancy of the Princess of Wales: 1981
- Prince William is born: 1982
- Charles and Diana move into Kensington Palace and Highgrove House: 1982
- Annual family Christmas luncheon: ongoing

In Her Own Words

"I cannot tell you how bloody awful it is. They call it morning sickness but I feel sick all the time." Diana, Princess of Wales.

Buckingham Palace Today:

This is a must-see if you are in London during the summer months. You can admire the Grand Staircase and visit many state rooms including the Green & White Drawing Rooms, Throne Room, Ballroom and State Dining Room. The Bow Room will lead you out to the back patio and extensive

---

gardens. Check times in advance to ensure you don't miss the Changing of the Guard. There are other special events on the calendar, so be sure to plan ahead.

I was lucky enough to attend a Royal Garden Party with my daughter, Robin in 2015. There are two held every year at Buckingham Palace hosted by the Queen and other members of the royal family. Approximately 8000 people attend – worthy members of various charities, military organizations and other nominated guests. As a Canadian, I was able to apply for a random lottery of available tickets and was lucky enough to win my own "golden ticket."

We shopped for elegant party dresses and fascinators (of course!) and booked our plane and hotel tickets for a whirlwind trip. I'd been to London a few times before, but this trip was extremely special as my daughter was living in Ghana at the time, so we both flew from opposite directions in the world to meet up in the U.K.

The Garden Party was absolutely incredible. It's a class act all the way. We arrived about an hour before the 4:00 p.m. start on a windy spring day. We joined thousands of other party-goers – all dressed in their finest, including uniforms and native dress from different parts of the world in addition to the rainbow colors of hats, dresses and formal suits.

Large white tents served the most exquisite sandwiches, desserts and tea that I've ever had. We had seconds and even thirds; everything was so delicious! I understand that Queen Elizabeth herself inspects the tents in advance to ensure all the details are perfect for her guests.

At precisely 4:00 p.m., two bands struck up *God Save The Queen* as Her Majesty, The Duke of Edinburgh, the Princess Royal and Princess Beatrice descended the steps. Other senior royals (Duke of Kent) also attended in top hat and tails. They each made their way down cordoned off laneways policed by Beefeaters from the Tower of London and plainclothes detectives. Pre-selected small groups of people were individually greeted by the Queen, who stopped to chat with them. She was dressed in a lovely pink suit and looked happy and cheerful.

At the end of the lanes, a VIP tent was set up for the royals and prestigious guests (not us!) where they enjoyed their own tea and refreshments. Then we had a free hour or so to wander the beautiful grounds and gardens and take lots of pictures.

At 6:00 p.m., the entire process was reversed as the royals made their way back up to the house through the lanes, smiling and waving as they slowly strolled past the guards. We probably got within three feet of Her Majesty and the Duke. They were smiling and looked content. The bands who had been playing throughout the party played the national anthem again as the royals disappeared into the palace. We left shortly thereafter. We had a fantastic time and it definitely stands out as one of my life's most memorable events! If you get the chance to attend one, don't miss it.

Whether you get an invitation a Garden Party or just a summer visit to Buckingham Palace, make your experience even more memorable by visiting the Buckingham Palace Shop across the road from the palace. I have spent many happy hours there browsing and shopping for official royal souvenirs that I use daily (teapots, dishes, towels, etc.) You can also order online at royalcollectionshop.co.uk. It's my favorite store in the world!

Visit rct.uk/visit/the-state-rooms-buckingham-palace
for opening times and visitor information.

2015 Royal Garden Party

NINE

Sandringham House

Norfolk, England
(Christmas holidays)

Sandringham is the other royal home, besides
Balmoral, that actually belongs to the Queen. The property
has stood in some form on its present site since the second
half of the eighteen-century. It's actually recorded in the in
the 1086 Domesday Book as Sant-Dersingham. Its royal
connection began in 1862 when Sandringham House and
8,000 acres were purchased from the Cowper family for
then-Prince of Wales, Albert (Queen Victoria's eldest son).

Prince Albert died the previous year but had made
provisions to purchase and restore the house for his son
and future King Edward VII.

After some renovations, the Prince of Wales moved into the home with his wife, Princess Alexandria of Denmark in 1863. As their family grew, additional houses were built: Bachelor's Cottage for guests and Park House which eventually ended up in the Spencer family and is discussed earlier in the book. Perhaps fate had a hand in bringing together Charles and Diana!

In 1870, the house was almost completely demolished and rebuilt to support a growing family. A ballroom and additional guest quarters were added some years later.

Sandringham is located in Norfolk, about a three-hour drive north from London, on the east coast. The property has been expanded to 20,000 acres and contains extensive gardens, a Transport Museum and St. Mary Magdelene church. The grounds are famous for royal shooting parties.

The house is made of red brick with limestone accents, and spans three stories including attics and a basement. The roof is tiled with multiple chimneys. A long drive unveils the house from the gatehouse.

The estate is open to the public, but only certain rooms are viewable. These include the Saloon, two Drawing Rooms, Dining Room, Gun Lobby & Ballroom Corridor, Ballroom and Museum. You can freely walk the gardens and visit the church.

When you enter the home, right away you see that it is a private residence and not a palace or castle. You pass through quite a small hallway before entering the heart of the house – the Saloon. You'll note the original weighing stool which was used in King Edward VII's era. Guests were weighed upon arrival and departure to prove they'd been well served with food and drink. It was expected that satisfied visitors gained several ounces during their stay!

The Saloon is two stories high with a coffered ceiling and Minstrel's Gallery. The room was used for balls and parties until the ballroom was built in 1881. Three large tapestries dot the walls depicting the life of the Roman Emperor, Constantine the Great. Many of the tapestries that serve as pillow and seat covers throughout the home were created by Queen Mary herself. A beautiful stone fireplace at the end of the room welcomes visitors to this warm space.

There are over 170 clocks in the house and a piece of Sandringham trivia is that King Edward VII had all the clocks set 30 minutes early. This was known as "Sandringham Time" so that the King and his guests could enjoy more daylight for shooting parties.

From here you can tour the two Drawing Rooms, Dining Room and Gun Lobby. Throughout you'll see cozy chairs and sofas alongside fine porcelains, sculptures and fine art – some are personal gifts to the royal family. The overall feeling is warm and comfortable.

The Gun Lobby displays many generations of the royal family's hunting guns. Along the walls, you'll see sketches and watercolours of various members of the royal family, including the present Duke of Edinburgh.

The Ballroom is over sixty feet long and thirty feet wide with three large glass chandeliers that originally hung at Buckingham Palace. The walls are decorated with oriental arms from the Prince of Wales' tour of India and far east. There is another minstrel's galley here which is used to project films when the Ballroom is converted to a cinema. The room is large enough for cocktail parties and other large estate events.

The Transport Museum was opened in 1930 and the stable block housing it was once used as the home for the Sandringham Fire Brigade. The royal garage forms part of the Museum and is a treat for car lovers. There are many vintage automobiles here including the first Royal car purchased by The Prince of Wales in 1900. Other notable cars include an impressive collection of shooting brakes including the 1924 Daimler that George V used at both Balmoral and Sandringham. There are also a number of model cars that have been presented to younger members of the Royal Family including an Aston Martin DB007 - a miniature replica of the James Bond Aston Martin car used in the films *Goldfinger* and *Thunderball* - complete with revolving license plate, bullet-proof screen, smoke discharger, water spray to deter pursuers, and concealed dummy machine guns. I can just imagine William and Harry as children thoroughly enjoying taking it for a spin.

Some state vehicles are also on display including Rolls Royces and the State Landau used for the opening of Parliament. You can see a 1939 fire engine and so much more! A photographic display of the Royal family since 1862 features in the Long Gallery. You'll have to look hard to spot a photo of Diana, Princess of Wales but I found a couple. Further rooms showcase other estate artifacts.

The sixty acres of gardens are lovely and expansive as they are at all royal properties. There are man-made lakes, a Woodland Walk, beautiful flower beds and unique sculptures. The circular walk takes you up to and around the house.

St. Mary Magdelene Church has been on site since the sixteenth century. It's a short walk from the house and is in regular use today by the royal family. It's the site of some famous noble baptisms, including Diana's in 1961 and Princess Charlotte's in 2015. Royal memorials and burials are also marked here.

Sandringham was the royal residence that was most familiar to Diana. Having grown up at Park House next door, she was occasionally exposed to the Queen and royal family. She was invited over at times to watch the movie *Chitty Chitty Bang Bang* with the royal children – an invitation she apparently resisted as boring. She played with Princes Andrew and Edward who were closest to her in age. She probably only saw Prince Charles at a distance from time to time.

As she grew into a young lady, this is probably where Diana drew the attention of the royal family as a prospective bride. Coming from an impeccable aristocratic pedigree, fresh-faced and unspoiled, Diana was literally the girl next door.

After she and Charles started dating in the summer of 1980, Diana was likely hoping for an invitation to the annual family Christmas at Sandringham. Sadly, she was disappointed. Traditionally, only the core royal family and their wives, husbands and children are invited. This has been slowly changing, as Meghan Markle was invited to Sandringham before she married Prince Harry.

The Queen and her family have been spending Christmas at Sandringham for many years. When the Queen's children were small, they spent some Christmases at Windsor Castle (where they also celebrate Easter), but royal Christmases returned permanently to Sandringham in 1988.

The Queen arrives first, a few days before Christmas. She takes the train from London to King's Lynn, where she is whisked to nearby Sandringham. The rest of the family arrives on Christmas Eve, in order of precedence. This means that the junior members of the family like Princesses Beatrice and Eugenie arrive first, followed by the Queen's children and families (e.g. the Princess Royal, the Duke of York and Earl of Wessex), and so on. The last to arrive are the senior royals: The Duke and Duchess of Cambridge, with George, Charlotte and Louis, and the Duke and Duchess of Cornwall, and the Queen and Prince Philip. They gather for afternoon tea in the saloon at 4:00 p.m. This includes finger sandwiches, scones with clotted cream and jam; and a ginger cake. The children finish decorating the Christmas tree but the job of placing the star at the top is reserved for Prince Philip. Inexpensive and jokey gifts are then exchanged before a formal dinner for adults with full finery – tuxedoes, gowns and jewelry – the works! French menus complement the candlelit dinner.

The next morning a buffet breakfast is served after the entire family receives stockings from the Queen, even the corgis. Then it's 11:00 mass following the famous walk to nearby St. Mary Magdalene Church, then drinks and nuts before Christmas luncheon. At 1:00 p.m. a turkey with all the trimmings in served to the adults after they open holiday crackers. A traditional Christmas pudding and brandy is lit and brought into the Dining Room for the grand finale. Then the family disperses until 3:00 when they assemble to watch the Queen's message on television. A full tea is served shortly thereafter.

Sandringham is renowned for being the location where King George V recorded his first radio Christmas message in 1932. This tradition has been carried on with subsequent monarchs, switching to television broadcasts in 1957. These royal messages were aired live from Sandringham until the Queen started pre-recording them from London in recent years. Millions of people listen to the Queen's royal message each Christmas Day to hear a brief summary of the year's events, family updates, and the Queen's holiday greetings.

A buffet dinner including hams, local game, vegetables and salads is served at 8:00 p.m. on Christmas night, although it's hard to imagine any of the family is still hungry. The family then relaxes with parlor games, puzzles and perhaps a song or two around the piano.

The next day the men head out early for the traditional Boxing Day pheasant shoot. The ladies join them for a hot lunch, before returning to the house for drinks and dinner. This pace continues until after the New Year, when the family slowly disperses, leaving the Queen and the Duke there until early February. Her Majesty stays until the anniversary of her father's death on February 6ᵗʰ.

Promptly at four p.m., after being shown their rooms and having changed, the family gathered in the White Drawing Room for tea. William and Harry were beyond excited.

"Did you see the table in the Red Drawing Room with all the presents, Mummy?" asked Harry, his blue eyes round with excitement. I found a pile with my name on it. It's huge! Can I open them?" Harry was jumping up and down.

"You have to wait until after tea," said William with the smug knowledge of an older brother.

Harry started to pout until Diana interjected. "But you can help Granny with the Christmas tree now, darling."

The invitation to holiday at Sandringham was essentially a royal command, so the entire family was there. The Queen and Prince Philip, The Queen Mother and Princess Margaret as the most senior royals were sipping tea. Princess Anne was there with her husband Captain Mark Philips. Their two children were placing ornaments on the tree. Prince Andrew was playing on the floor with the Princesses Beatrice and Eugenie. Fergie was chatting with Prince Philip. And young Prince Edward was throwing a ball to the dogs by the fireplace. It seemed a cozy scene, albeit it all of the younger royal marriages were in trouble. It was reputed that Anne and Mark were barely on speaking terms and it showed. Andrew and Sarah studiously ignored each other. And Charles and Diana busied themselves in separate activities – Diana with the boys, whilst Charles greeted his mother.

After tea, the royal family opened gifts according to tradition. Diana had been shocked when she'd initially brought cashmere sweaters and silk ties to the first gathering in 1981. Surprisingly, the family exchanged modest gifts – some might have even said cheap. Gag gifts were all the rage – especially for the men. It had taken a bit of getting used to, but she had gotten into the spirit and relished finding chic and funny gifts for everyone on Kensington High Street. From Diana, A Spencer in Turmoil.

Diana attended her first Sandringham Christmas as Princess of Wales in 1981, when she was three months pregnant. A famous incident saw the Princess either fall or throw herself down a small staircase, depending on who is telling the story. Diana claimed in *Diana, Her True Story* that she deliberately hurled herself down the stairs in a desperate bid for attention and cry for help. Others have claimed it was a simple slip on the stairs. Regardless, the Queen was nearby and understandably alarmed. The doctor was called, and Diana and the baby were proclaimed to be fine. Charles went out shooting which Diana later claimed he did in distaste and indifference.

Subsequently, Diana spent every Christmas at Sandringham with Prince Charles and her growing family until the separation in 1992. She claimed to find it a stuffy and claustrophobic experience where she tended to spend her time with the children, talking to staff in the kitchens, and on her phone speaking to friends for moral support.

Sadly, one of these phone calls was later exposed in the *Squidgygate* scandal of 1992. In approximately 1989, Diana was speaking to her friend James Gilbey from Sandringham. The tape was leaked to the press – either by a local ham operator or someone spying on the Princess depending on who you believe – but deemed too explosive to publicize.

Diana's last official Christmas at Sandringham was in 1991, a year before the separation. She probably heaved a massive sigh of relief to leave behind the formal traditions and conventional celebrations of the Victorian family Christmas as happily as she bade goodbye to Balmoral and Buckingham Palace. She attended one or two other Christmas Eve get-togethers at Sandringham, but departed early on Christmas Day.

In subsequent years, Diana would jet to a warm holiday in the Caribbean with friends at Christmastime, leaving William and Harry with Charles. Undoubtably, this was bittersweet for the Mum who dearly loved her boys.

Sandringham has remained the private country home – typically for Christmas holidays – for four generations of sovereigns: King Edward VII, King George V, King George VI and our present monarch, Queen Elizabeth II.

Sandringham House

St. Mary Magdelene Church

Significant Events that happened at Sandringham

- Diana Spencer was baptized at St. Mary Magdelene Church, 1961
- Diana falls down the stairs while pregnant with William: 1982
- *Squidgygate* tape recorded: 1989
- Diana's last Christmas at Sandringham: 1991

In Her Own Words
"There was really something strange; I was leaning over the fence yesterday, looking into Park House, and I thought: 'Oh, what shall I do?' And I thought: 'Well, my friend would say go in and do it,' I thought: 'No, 'cause I am a bit shy,' and there were hundreds of people in there. So I thought: 'Bugger that.' So I walked round to the front door, and walked straight in." [Park

House, former Spencer home, where Diana once lived, had become Leonard Cheshire home for the disabled.] *"It was just so exciting. And they were so sweet. They wanted their photographs taken with me, and they kept hugging me. They were very ill, some of them. Some no legs, and all sorts of things."* Diana, Princess of Wales.

Sandringham House Today

Sandringham is open to tourists from April to October. It's about a two-hour train trip from London plus a fifteen-minute taxi from King's Lynn station. You'll probably spend about a half-day at the estate and can find Bed and Breakfast accommodations in King's Lynn.

Entering through the main gate, you can approach the house via the wide driveway. Inside, you can tour the Saloon, Small & Large Drawing Rooms, Dining Room, Gun Lobby & Ballroom Corridor, and Ballroom. Outside you can visit the Museum and gardens. There are helpful guides in all the rooms. Be sure to ask them questions!

After you tour the house, be sure to take the walk to St. Mary Magdelene Church. You can recreate the annual Christmas stroll that the royals take from the house to the arbor archway and through to the tiny church. Sit and take in the ambience and imagine generations of royal mothers (including Diana) shushing small children during the Christmas service.

When I visited in 2019, I found something quite special about the walk to the house. The sound of mourning doves cooing serenaded me. I'm not sure it this is a normal occurrence or something that just happened on that fine, summer day, but it was quite magical.

Of all the royal residences I've visited, this one was the most reminiscent of Downton Abbey. It's a large country estate, but not as massive as royal palaces. The inside rooms are spacious, but also comfy and cozy. It's obviously a family home. I could almost see Lord and Lady Grantham making a visit to the Queen for a Christmas drink.

Anmer Hall on the estate is not open to the public but is the country home of the Duke and Duchess of Cambridge. You might see William, Kate and their children playing outside when the children are on school break.

His Royal Highness, The Duke of Edinburgh has retired from public life and currently lives on Wood Farm on the Sandringham estate.

When you get back to the front gates, walk across the road to the gift shop and cafe for shopping and refreshment. I spent about an hour in the gift shop, buying souvenirs and flower seeds for my garden.

Visit <u>sandringhamestate.co.uk</u> for opening times and visitor information.

TEN

Highgrove House

Gloucestershire, England
(1982 – 1992)

Diana first visited Highgrove House in the late summer or early fall of 1981, while dating the Prince. He had recently bought the estate as a country home, and was in the process of remodeling and redecorating it.

The location was ideal – a short two-hour drive from London, near his sister Anne's country home of Gatcombe, and only about a fifteen-minute drive from the country home of his good friends – Andrew and Camilla Parker-Bowles.

Originally built in the late 18th century as "High Grove," it had changed hands several times and even been partially reconstructed after a fire. The Duchy of Cornwall had purchased it in 1980 from Maurice MacMillan, the son of former British Prime Minister Harold MacMillan, on behalf of Prince Charles.

Set in over five hundred acres southwest of Tetbury in Gloucestershire, Highgrove was the perfect location for a country home for the young Prince. Located in the heart of the Beaufort Hunt, it was ideal for Charles' shooting and polo passions.

Highgrove is a grey rectangular building with a stone and slate roof in the neo-classical style. Three stories high, with a squarish stone exterior, it resembles an upscale version of a "chocolate box house" – one that graces the lid of a traditional box of chocolates. Small by royal house standards, it is stately in its own right. Flowers and ivy were encouraged to grow up the exterior walls. Looking out from the front of the house, you can see St. Mary's parish church in local Tetbury. One of Highgrove's previous owners paid for the rebuilding of the church so that he and his successors would always have a clear and amazing view of it. Highgrove is also the location of Home Farm, now an extensive example of organic farming, gardening and wildlife.

In Diana's time, visitors saw a round table in the middle of the hallway with an impressive dried flower arrangement. With four main reception rooms, nine bedrooms with ensuite bathrooms, a nursery wing, and staff and security quarters, it was large but not enormous. There was also a fully-stocked and well-hidden safe room to be used by the royals and staff in the event of a severe security threat. It contained sleeping facilities, food and other amenities needed to withstand at least a thirty-day emergency.

The interior was decorated with light yellow walls, cane furniture, with wooden floors and green carpets. Rooms were decorated with many photographs of William and Harry, as well as the Prince's own watercolors and Wemyss pottery. Plants of many types and fresh flowers abounded in each room.

Aside from the typical sitting room, drawing room and kitchens, a focal point of the main floor was the Prince's library. Books and papers were piled everywhere, and he spent many hours working on speeches and royal correspondence while listening to music and looking out to the terrace and gardens. Staff were under strict instructions to leave any and all piles undisturbed.

Diana's bedroom and sitting room were decorated in the light pastels and chintzes that she favored overall. A comfy sofa was home to dozens of her stuffed animals including teddy bears, frogs and penguins. Knick-knacks, ornaments and photos topped every open surface in both rooms.

The Prince had his own sitting and bathroom decorated in a more muted style. His own shabby Teddy took pride of place on the bed when Charles was in residence. As the marriage broke down, he would sleep in his sitting room.

By far the most stunning and impressive aspect of the home was (and is) the gardens – Prince Charles' pride and joy! He had expanded on the original grounds to add a Sundial garden, Thyme Walk, a walled kitchen garden, Woodland retreat, and so much more. It was his solace and hideaway, and he loved nothing more than to spend hours digging, planting and conferring with his groundskeepers to continually enlarge and expand it. It now boasts a Cottage Garden, Oak Pavilion, Wildflower Meadow, Azalea Walk, Winterbourne Garden, Stumpery, Carpet Garden and an Arboretum Sanctuary. The young princes frequently played army games in the thatched treehouse known as *Hollyrood House* (a play on the royal Scottish Holyrood Palace) – built on an oak platform, supported by shards of Welsh slate and limestone steps.

Charles had proudly shown Diana his new country estate during their dating days and asked the young girl to help decorate the interior. Although initially daunted by the request, the teenager had risen to the occasion and with the help of her mother's designer Dudley Poplak had turned the large country home in a cozy and elegant entertainment hub for the country set. She had integrated a multitude of unique wedding presents into the Highgrove design just as she had for the KP redesign project. The overall effect was light, comfortable, and modern. From Diana, A Spencer in Turmoil.

Once Charles and Diana were engaged, Diana had begun the redesign and redecoration of both Highgrove and Kensington Palace.

It's hard to imagine a newlywed royal, being inundated in her new role, pregnant and extremely ill with morning sickness – and decorating two large homes. All at the tender age of twenty! Not much is written about this time in Diana's life, but I can only guess at how overwhelming it was for her. Especially when she was also fighting (and hiding!) her bulimia, and slowly realizing that her husband was still in love with another woman – Camilla Parker-Bowles.

After an extended honeymoon that included the obligatory summer retreat to Balmoral Castle with the rest of the family, Charles and Diana moved back to Charles' suite at Buckingham Palace until both new homes were ready.

Charles and his family were perplexed and concerned with the new bride. The fun and cheerful girl was gone. In her place was a thin, tearful, nervous and unpredictable young woman who spent inordinate amounts of time in her room and on the phone to her friends. The Windsors didn't understand what had happened.

To understand many of the royal family's actions and reactions - then and even now - it's important to recognize just how damaging the abdication of 1936 had been. Queen Elizabeth's uncle David, King Edward VIII, had fallen madly in love with an American commoner and divorcee, and was determined to marry her. Wallis Simpson was a Baltimore socialite who had caught the King's eye when he was Prince of Wales – even though she was still married to her second husband, Ernest Simpson.

David (as the family called him) was obsessed with Wallis, and a public outcry quickly followed. Although hushed up in the U.K., David's parents King George V and Queen Mary were shocked, appalled and outraged that the heir to the throne was getting serious about an American divorcee. It was one thing to have her as a mistress, but to consider her as a wife (and Queen Consort!) was out of the question.

After the King died, David succeeded him as King Edward VIII. He continued to try to work with the British parliament to find a way to make Wallis his wife, all to no avail. After just ten months as King, David abdicated to be with the woman he loved.

It's widely known in royal circles that David was ambivalent about becoming the monarch. He was excited about the potential to make a big impact, but chafed at the required duties and responsibilities. Some people believe that he grasped on to the Wallis situation to neatly sidestep the crown, and have the woman he loved. After the abdication and a short waiting period while Wallis's second divorce was finalized, the two married. They were named the Duke and Duchess of Windsor. They lived an aimless life, mainly in Paris, and the Duke never took up royal duties in England again. During World War II, he eagerly sought an official role to help the Allies. He was named Governor of The Bahamas in 1940. He and Wallis spent the next five years there.

With David abdicating, it was left to his brother, the Duke of York Albert (Bertie) to take on the enormous task of King. This he did, with the steadfast support of his wife, the popular Duchess of York (Elizabeth). They had to face an extremely challenging reign throughout World War II. Bertie took on the name King George VI to help restore the image of stability to the monarchy, and became a remarkable King. Unfortunately, he died prematurely of prolonged stress and lung cancer at the age of 56. Queen Elizabeth, the Queen Mother never forgave the Duke and Duchess of Windsor again.

It was through this abdication crisis that Queen Elizabeth II became the heir to the throne after her father. She grew up from a young age knowing she would be Queen, and was well trained by King George VI to take up her royal duties. It was never expected that she would succeed so early – at the young age of twenty-five - as a young wife and mother herself.

The entire House of Windsor was rocked by this abdication controversy and was determined to never have any whiff of scandal touch the monarchy again. The young Queen even refused her younger sister Princess Margaret's request to marry her true love, Group Captain Peter Townsend because he was divorced.

All potential royal spouses were vetted scrupulously, and even Prince Charles himself delayed and deferred marriage until the age of thirty-two – partly because he was terrified to make the wrong choice. It was imperative that he not get it wrong, nor repeat the mistake of his great-uncle David.

So, you can understand why the Queen, Prince Philip and Prince Charles were distressed and dismayed that this pliable young Spencer girl had turned into a sulky, emotional wreck – on her honeymoon!

Almost every action and decision taken by the House of Windsor has been colored with the black paintbrush of the 1936 abdication, so when you look at how the royal family responded to Princess Diana, you will understand their behavior.

It's ironic, then, that the second most frightening threat to the monarchy in the 20th century occurred the week after the Princess of Wales died – when all of England was angry and outraged at the lack of support and visible grief from the Queen and her immediate family. It was only when the monarch travelled down early from Balmoral, flew a Union Jack at half-mast at Buckingham Palace, and spoke live to the nation that harmony and goodwill was restored. The crisis was narrowly averted.

It's important to understand this background when trying to appreciate what the Queen and royal family did to help the young Princess of Wales in the early years. Everything was done in the service of accommodating the young bride and ensuring stability in the royal marriage.

After the Balmoral honeymoon, Charles and Diana moved back to Buckingham Palace while their two residences were being renovated.

At this time, Charles was having serious concerns about his new wife and her emotional outbursts, rampant bulimia and obvious unhappiness. He had her visit a number of psychologists and psychiatrists in that fall of 1981. Although they diagnosed various conditions such as anxiety and depression, Diana refused to take any anti-depressants.

The Prince and Princess made their first visit to Wales where Diana charmed everyone – despite being pregnant and ill with morning sickness. Once it was announced that the Princess was expecting the next heir to the British throne, there was great rejoicing in the land. And behind palace doors, there were also enormous sighs of relief. So, this was what had made Diana so unhappy and emotional…the hormones of pregnancy! The whole world expected her to return to her happy and well-adjusted state as soon as she settled into pregnancy and when the baby was born.

That Christmas, Diana spent her first royal holiday at Sandringham with the entire family. This was a "must-show" for all of them – and there's even an order of precedence. Each royal's arrival is timed based on their position and seniority in the royal family – with the Queen and the Duke as senior hosts.

Christmas at Sandringham in Norfolk would have been a bittersweet experience for the young Princess. The estate was right next door to her childhood home of Park House, which would have certainly brought back lots of memories. But of course, none of the Spencers lived there anymore, so Diana would have had to make do with the "big house."

Traditions at Sandringham were historic and remain virtually unchanged to this day. There's a combination of informal family time and gift-giving, combined with formal dinners with full evening dress; and the walk to church on Christmas Day at local St. Mary Magdalene. Likely, it would have been slightly intimidating for this young bride, but I'm sure Diana rose to the challenge – despite her discomfort with large groups & her ongoing morning sickness.

Charles and Diana moved into Highgrove in the spring of 1982, a few months before Prince William's birth.

Kensington Palace was ready shortly after and it became the official residence of the Prince and Princess of Wales.

Highgrove became the weekend sanctuary for the Wales', and they stayed there most weekends for most of their marriage when not travelling. It was an oasis in the midst of two hectic lives. Depending on the royal, they each attended a minimum of 200-300 engagements per year – in London, "awaydays" across the UK, and extensive overseas trips and state visits. Highgrove afforded the young couple a place to relax, entertain friends and enjoy nature.

Charles continued with his outdoors activities as he had as a single man: local fox hunts, riding, hiking and a full schedule of polo – both practices and matches. Any spare time was spent (as it now) working on the Highgrove gardens – creating new designs and garden beds, conferring with the head gardener, and even planting, pruning and weeding himself.

Diana loved the swimming pool at Highgrove, and in good weather she swam lengths each morning. It was also the site of many afternoon swim parties over the years. The Princess wasn't as keen on outdoor pursuits, although she did show an interest in the gardens in the early years. She preferred shopping with the boys in local Tetbury or Cirencester, or talking on the phone with friends. She also took long, solitary walks with her Walkman plastered to her head, and enjoyed afternoons or evenings listening to music.

Together, the royal couple entertained regularly. Whether it was the wide circle of the Prince's friends, family on both sides or visiting dignitaries, Highgrove was always a hub of guests – both dinner and overnight. Diana never warmed up to Charles's friends – who she called cronies or the "Highgrove set" – because she thought they were old, sycophantic to the Prince, and with whom she shared no common interests. She was bored by them. Similarly, Charles didn't have much use for Diana's young, aristocratic friends who he found lightweight and shallow. So unfortunately, even from the early days in their marriage, Charles and Diana led separate lives.

Because it was such a warm night, they took their afters on the terrace with coffee and drinks.

"Well, what's it to be girls? Charades? Bridge? Dancing to music?" Fergie wanted to liven up the party.

The girls couldn't agree so drifted back to the sitting room to decide.

"After being so scheduled and told what to do for ten years, I just like to relax and do nothing sometimes." Diana stretched out on the sofa. She was a little tipsy, and smiled at her dear friends. "Although this one" – she pointed at Fergie – "always gets me into trouble with the in-laws. Remember when we dressed up as policemen to crash Andrew's bachelor party? We almost got arrested ourselves for impersonating officers. Luckily, the PPOs recognised and rescued us." Diana felt the giggles coming on.

"Well I just wanted to check that Andrew was behaving himself before the wedding. And lucky for him – he was, the bugger." Fergie was laughing too.

"We've had some good – and bad times – over the years, haven't we Fergie? Diana asked wistfully. From Diana, A Spencer in Turmoil

Frequent visitors to Highgrove were Andrew and Camilla Parker-Bowles who had a country home – Bolehyde Manor – a mere twelve miles away. Andrew was an army man that knew Charles from polo. He and Camilla had two young children.

Of course, it's well known that Camilla and Charles had been lovers in the 1970s. Although Charles had been deeply in love with Camilla, she was unsuitable to be a royal wife because of her romantic past, and was probably not quite aristocratic enough to suit the Windsors. Charles went to sea for a six-month tour with the Navy and in the meantime, Camilla married the eligible Parker-Bowles. Charles and Camilla remained good friends as Charles continued to date and search for a suitable bride.

About five years later, Charles and Camilla became lovers again after the death of Lord Louis Mountbatten – a mentor and father figure to the young prince. Charles had been devastated by the loss of his great-uncle, and Camilla was a great comfort to him. Reportedly, the two reconnected their physical relationship at this time.

After Charles' engagement to Diana, he and Camilla halted their ongoing affair, although they remained the best of friends. Camilla even helped Charles draw up a list of eligible young aristocrats to take on the daunting job of Princess of Wales. Lady Diana Spencer was at the top of the list.

Diana had suspicions about this close "friend" of her fiancé, which triggered the onset of her bulimia during the engagement. She became obsessed with the other woman which caused a huge and ongoing rift between her and her husband. Charles refused to give up Camilla's friendship. Whenever Andrew and Camilla visited the Wales' at Highgrove, Diana would make herself scarce. She couldn't stand to be around the older woman.

But, back in June 1982, William's birth brought the young royal couple together as parents. They both doted on young William and were connected as a couple in a wonderful way. Unfortunately, Diana suffered post-partum depression and struggled to overcome it on her own, while still fighting bulimia. Harry's birth in 1984 completed the young family, and Diana was quoted as saying that this was the happiest time in the royal marriage. She had delivered the "heir and the spare" who were both healthy and happy.

Weekends at Highgrove now took on a regular pattern. Diana arrived with the nursery (nanny and children), plus her own dresser (a modern-day stylist) and security staff – usually on Friday nights or Saturdays. Charles would arrive (often via the Queen's Flight helicopter) as soon as he was free from his engagements. Charles and the children would play outside, or swim with Diana. The couple would dine alone after Diana and the nanny bathed the boys and put them to bed on the rare occasions that they had no guests. As the princes grew, Diana would also take them shopping in Tetbury and watch videos with them in bed at night.

Highgrove had a full staff to look after the young family: Wendy Berry, the housekeeper, Paul Burrell, the butler (and eventual KP butler and confidante to the Princess), chefs, daily cleaners, security and gardening staff. It was a bustling household.

William and Harry adored Highgrove and the endless pursuits available to them. They both had a fascination for army games which they played all over the estate – complete with miniature army fatigues and toy guns. They took weekly riding lessons from the estate groom and took turns riding Smokey the pony. They loved to drive around in a donated green miniature Aston Martin, with William as chief driver. They even had their own woodshed full of multi-colored plastic balls to jump and play in. And they played often with the Burrell's boys – Nick and Alex – who were of a similar age. It was an idyllic childhood for them, and a great break away from London and the press.

Around 1986, Charles and Camilla resumed their romantic relationship. Allegedly, Prince Philip insisted that Charles give the marriage 100% effort for five years, including giving up his mistress. Charles agreed. I believe he truly tried to make the marriage work to the best of his ability. But by 1986, Diana and Charles were not sleeping together any longer, and fought constantly.

It was during this period that Charles and Diana's Highgrove routine changed. Diana still came most weekends with Harry (William was at boarding school) but usually only for one night. She planned events for herself and Harry that were separate from Charles. He joined the little family later and stayed on at Highgrove after Diana returned to London after Sunday lunch. He now regularly spent Sunday nights and other weekdays with Camilla – either at Highgrove or her own country home.

Diana began her affair with Major James Hewitt sometime after this period and he was a regular Highgrove visitor when the prince was away. He got to know both William and Harry quite well, and they looked up to Uncle Jamie for his army status.

As the royal marriage slowly deteriorated, Diana spent less and less time at Highgrove. Stopping there for barely twenty-four hours on most weekends, she tried to avoid Charles as much as possible and often times, they missed each other by minutes on the road between Highgrove and Kensington Palace. Highgrove became Charles' unofficial main residence and he spent as much time as possible at the estate throughout the week. When Diana was not there, Camilla played regular hostess to Charles and his friends. Staff knew her as the chatelaine of Highgrove as she and Charles hosted many house parties and guests as a couple.

After the official separation of Charles and Diana in December of 1992, Diana made one last visit to Highgrove to retrieve her personal items – photos, teddy bears, clothing, etc. She was awarded the use of the Kensington

Palace apartments as part of the settlement and she stayed there until her death. She never returned to Highgrove.

Significant Events that happened at Highgrove House

- Prince Charles and Princess Diana finish decorating the home and begin to use it as their regular weekend retreat and entertaining space: 1982
- The Prince & Princess stop coming together for weekends: 1987 (approximately)
- Charles breaks his arm at polo and convalesces at Highgrove for the summer: 1990
- The first excerpts of *Diana, Her True Story* are published in the *Sunday Times* and faxed to Prince Charles at Highgrove: 1992
- After the formal separation is announced, Diana retrieves her personal belongings and leaves Highgrove forever: 1992

In Her Own Words
"It is extremely wet in Gloucestershire. In fact, it seems to rain all the time. It's a wonderful place for the boys and my husband with all its outdoor things, but I'm afraid it's not really my cup of tea." Diana, Princess of Wales.

Highgrove House Today:
If you get the chance to visit Highgrove House in Gloucestershire, you won't be disappointed. It does take some organization and planning to get there – from London it's at least two train rides plus a taxi.

HRH, Prince Charles and Camilla, Duchess of Cornwall spend most weekends at Highgrove, so it's only open for a limited time in the summer while the royals holiday at Balmoral in Scotland.

You can't see the actual house, but the garden tour is nothing short of spectacular. It takes about two hours and you'll see the thirty-plus years of love and attention that the Prince of Wales has invested in the many gardens. The guided tour is followed by an elegant and delicious champagne tea, accompanied by live music.

I visited in 2018 and loved it. I was thrilled to be walking the grounds where Princess Diana and the boys laughed and played. Near the beginning of the tour, we were taken quite close to the house itself and I couldn't help looking up into the windows facing the Thyme Walk – almost seeing Diana peering through the curtains. The various different garden sections are imaginative and unique – I particularly liked the walled garden and seeing William and Harry's old treehouse. I wonder if George, Charlotte and Louis use it now?

The tour guides are knowledgeable and shared lots of stories about the Prince's projects and endeavors – he is world-renowned for his passion for organic gardening and farming. It really is breathtaking.

Of course, you can purchase souvenirs and garden mementos at the gift shop. Check highgrovegardens.com for opening times and visitor information.

The author at Highgrove House 2018

ELEVEN

Kensington Palace

London, England
(1982 – 1997)

Not long after Diana finished redecorating and the newlyweds moved into Highgrove, their London home was ready – Kensington Palace. Nicknamed KP, it was their London base for all activities and entertaining for the length of their marriage, and Diana's home until her death.

The Queen gave Charles and Diana the refurbished and combined L-shaped three-storied Apartments 8 and 9. Set in the heart of London in the fashionable and wealthy Knightsbridge district, it abuts Millionaire's Row on Kensington Palace Gardens which is home to some of Britain's wealthiest homeowners. The average home there is worth over $35 million dollars.

Kensington Palace is a large compound that comprises a number of grace and favor homes for the Queen's relatives, as well as public rooms open for viewing, The Orangery restaurant and Kensington Gardens. Grace and favor homes house senior royals, active and retired staff in good standing and others that the Queen has decided to honor with a home in an exclusive location with little or no rent.

Sometimes known as the aunt heap, the Palace also housed other senior royals in their own grace-and-favour apartments – homes bestowed by the Queen for nominal or low rents in exchange for service or familial proximity to the crown. Queen Victoria had been born at KP, and the Duke and Duchess of Gloucester were neighbours of Charles and Diana. Prince and Princess Michael of Kent also called Kensington Palace home as did perhaps the most famous resident – HRH, Princess Margaret. The Queen's sister lived at #10. Many retired staff lived in more humble accommodations or cottages as well. Diana's sister Jane, who was married to the Queen's private secretary Robert Fellowes, had been given a cottage on the grounds – The Old Barracks. There was often the sound of the Spencer cousins playing in the Kensington Palace courtyard. From Diana, A Spencer in Turmoil.

In total, KP housed over a hundred people and four royal households living independently with their own staffs: private secretaries, equerries, ladies-in-waiting, butlers, housekeepers, chauffeurs, maids, dressers, and security (known as Personal Protection Officers or PPOs). Most rarely saw each other and had no daily contact.

Numbers 8 and 9 were tucked behind the palace front, on the north side, facing a small green, and out of sight and access to the public.

Diana enjoyed her own private walled garden, and according to her butler Paul Burrell, in *A Royal Duty*, she delighted in sunbathing, listening to music and reading here on warm summer days. You can imagine she played there with Princes William and Harry, enjoying picnics and chasing each other around.

Built in 1689, the red-bricked Palace is located in central London just off Kensington High Street – one of Diana's favorite places to shop for the boys' clothing and gifts for friends and family.

King William the III had been KP's first royal inhabitant. Queen Victoria had spent her sheltered childhood at the palace, and it was here that she was informed at age eighteen that she was now Queen of England. She then moved to Buckingham Palace for the remainder of her long reign.

Kitchens, staff and security rooms were located on the lower ground floor with receptions rooms found at street level. Bedrooms, family space and guest rooms occupied the second floor. The cheery yellow-painted nursery was housed in the attic space on the third level.

Diana had hired her mother's decorator Dudley Poplak to help her design KP as well as Highgrove. She had tried to integrate as many wedding gifts as possible into both homes, as well borrowing pieces of art and furniture from the Royal Collection. She later claimed that decorating both of these homes saved her sanity in the first hectic months of her marriage.

For the public area, a main feature was a large reception room that could comfortably seat seventy-five guests. Charles and Diana rarely used this space, preferring the drawing room for more intimate gatherings of fifteen or so visitors. This floor boasted a library and two dining rooms as well. The formal dining space could easily seat sixteen around a unique round mahogany table. It was used to entertain visiting dignitaries, royal family members, charity executives, and other important guests.

The overall feeling was elegant and gracious – if a little dark. Very little natural light was let in, and some of the rooms and corridors were small, giving a sense of being cramped – despite Diana and Dudley's best design efforts.

A sweeping white Georgian staircase led to the family space upstairs. A large master bedroom with a custom-made four-poster bed that had been built for King Edward VII occupied a prime spot. Completely covered with Diana's cuddly toys and Charles' boyhood battered but beloved Teddy, it was an odd juxtaposition of historic royalty and childish keepsakes. There were two dressing rooms with accompanying bathrooms. Charles often slept on the single bed in his own dressing room – especially as the marriage unraveled over the years.

The drawing room was large, and decorated with ornate carpets, formal window coverings, and painted yellow like the front hall. Two green sofas faced each other in a family grouping near the marble fireplace. A piano stood in the corner and was played by Diana – occasionally for friends - but mostly for herself. A large Flemish tapestry took up most of the wall opposite the sofas and was a focal point for the room. The Georgian windows overlooked the back of the sprawling palace.

Diana's private sitting room was her oasis of dusty pinks and light blues. The sofas were covered with light floral chintz. The Princess was often found sitting at her lady's desk penning thank you notes to friends and party hosts on her personalized Diana stationery embossed with a crown and her name.

Circular tables dotted the room and were covered with fine blue silk tablecloths and dozens of framed photographs of William and Harry. Other pictures of beloved family members like her father the Earl, and photos taken with celebrities like Elton John and Liza Minnelli cluttered the tables and walls. Built-in cabinets and bureau tops were crammed with her Herend glass animal collection, stuffed animals, children's drawings, and other bits and pieces like embroidered cushions with sayings like "You have to kiss a lot of frogs before you find a Prince." Diana kept the room filled with her favorite lilies and warm candles. An area rug set off the furniture groupings. It was a cozy and girlish chamber. Diana spent much of her time alone there.

The young princes were also comfortable in the sitting room, lounging on an overstuffed leather and fur hippo cushion in front of the fireplace watching television or doing homework.

Charles' sitting room, by contrast, was quite masculine. Dark and rich furniture was cluttered with an eclectic assortment of books, work papers and priceless objects. Piles of paperwork littered the carpet in a similar chaotic fashion as his Highgrove study.

On his desk stood a large photograph of the Prince with his father the Duke of Edinburgh, ironically inscribed by Charles himself – "I was not born to follow in my father's footsteps." Charles spent many a long evening in this room dealing with mountains of paperwork sent over by both Buckingham and St. James Palaces. He preferred to work quietly and often shooed the boys out when they bounced in for roughhousing games.

I can only imagine how relieved Diana must have been to finally move into her London home in the spring of 1982 just before William was born. Staying with Charles in the Prince's Buck House bachelor apartments was probably slightly cramped and would have reminded the Princess of her husband's pre-wedding life – without her. Like any new wife, I'm sure she welcomed the opportunity to have her own new home to get a fresh start for her marriage.

At this time, Diana was still overwhelmed with her new royal life – getting used to a hectic schedule of engagements, trying to deal with an insatiable press and a public that seemed only to gain interest in her after her marriage. She was secretly fighting the bulimia that she would battle for the better part of ten years, pregnant with her first child, and trying to make her new marriage work, while knowing her husband's affections were divided at best, dedicated to another women at worst. Poor Diana!

At first Diana's public engagements were limited to accompanying Charles to his pre-set openings, dinners, official royal events, and overseas tours. She was terrified in public, tongue-tied with officials and celebrities, and was absolutely petrified of public speaking. She wanted to support her husband, but found it difficult to cope with her new life. Many times, Charles or staff had to encourage and reassure the panicked young Princess to get out of the car at an official engagement.

Her first tour with the Prince of Wales was a three-day visit to Wales in October 1981. Although pregnant at the time, it wasn't officially known, and the Princess struggled to keep up her duties with massive crowds meeting them everywhere. This is where it first started that the people wanted to see Diana, not Charles. Neither of them understood this – Charles was the Prince of Wales and would one day be King. Diana was a twenty-year old uneducated young Sloane – famous only for marrying the Prince. Charles had lived his life in the spotlight, adored by people around the world, his every whim indulged by staff and friends, the love of many woman at his disposal. It's understandable that he was self-centered and self-absorbed – he's been surrounded by sycophants his entire life. He must have been shocked and appalled to be relegated to second-place or even ignored. Diana herself was horrified at all the attention focused on her – she just wanted to be a good wife and supporter to her husband.

But the press and public were voracious and insatiable. This obsession with Diana continued, unabated and unchecked until her death. It endures even twenty-plus years after her death. Back in 1981, it was a crucial blow to the young marriage of the Prince and Princess of Wales – a blow that could never be overcome.

Despite horrific morning sickness, Diana valiantly carried on with her new duties and engagements.

All new royals joining the family are encouraged to take on charities and patronages to suit their personal interests. Their lives are centered around service and supporting hundreds of charities and military organizations. In this capacity, they represent the U.K. locally and around the world, and literally raise millions of dollars every year for many worthy causes. At first, Diana stuck with what she knew and loved – children and the elderly - and became a patron of *Barnardo's* and *Help the Aged.* She even learned sign language when she took on the *British Deaf Association.*

As time went on, she picked up more and more charities. With her passion for dance, it was natural for her to champion the *London City Ballet.* She also began to gravitate towards less popular charities – those that helped the most neglected, the sickest, the poorest and the neediest in society. Over the years, she became patrons of hospitals, homeless shelters, AIDS groups, and many others. Before she gave her famous "time and space" speech after the formal separation, she was president or patron of over 100 charities. I would love to know how much money she raised for all these worthy causes. Just having her attend a dinner would raise the entry prices and the event would be sold out. Fundraising flourished if her name was attached to a charity, and when she attended their functions. The papers would be full of photos and stories the day after any major event. She truly made a major impact on so many people and important issues.

June 21, 1982 was a big day for Diana, Charles, the royal family and England. Prince William Arthur Philip Louis was born at 9:03 p.m. at the Lindo Wing of St. Mary's Hospital in London and became the second in line to the British throne. Diana had wanted to deliver in hospital, rather than at home, as was the royal custom at the time. The Princess of Wales won that battle – as well as the one over Prince William's name. Apparently, Charles wanted him to be called Arthur or Albert, but Diana stood firm for William.

Diana was in labor for about twelve hours and had a natural birth, with an epidural for the pain. The world rejoiced at the birth of healthy boy (7 lb. 1 oz.) and heir. Prince Charles was mobbed on the street when he appeared a few hours later.

Diana further shocked the world when she appeared on the steps of the Lindo Wing a mere twenty-four hours later. Remember, this was 1982 and new moms typically stayed in hospital for three-five days after a normal birth. So, for the Princess of Wales to leave the hospital a day after having a baby was nothing short of revolutionary at the time. But Diana was a young, healthy woman and knew that she wanted to be home with her new infant son. She breastfed for a couple of months and insisted on spending hours per day bonding with her baby that she adored.

In later years, Diana would be called *The Mouse That Roared* and I think if you trace back her actions and attitudes right to the early days of her marriage, you'll see that she was always a strong-minded woman who fought to get her own way, based upon her instincts.

Diana was a devoted mother, determined to shower the love and affection on William that she lacked in her own childhood. She never faltered in this till the day she died – always prioritizing both William and Harry, spending as much time with them as possible, and nurturing them in their challenging and difficult roles in the public spotlight. And she always strived to create a "normal" childhood for them, taking them shopping and to outings normally forbidden to royal children like amusement parks and Disneyland.

Unfortunately, Diana struggled with post-partum depression after William's birth. She loved her son dearly and soldiered on with her royal engagements. Pictures of her after William's birth show her shockingly thin, so her bulimia was probably rampant at this time.

I think Diana was slowly starting to realize that her expectations of marriage were not going to be fulfilled. She wanted and needed a husband who was utterly devoted to her and their son. She pushed Charles to cut back on his commitments to spend more time as a family. The Prince tried to make time each day for his young family, but it was never enough. As Prince of Wales and heir, his schedule was jam-packed, and he simply couldn't abandon his responsibilities – even if he wanted to. And I doubt he even considered it. He was raised to do his duty no matter what, and I'm sure the demands of his young, unpredictable and emotional wife were baffling and astonishing to him. He just couldn't understand her.

For her part, Diana couldn't fathom why her new husband didn't want to spend more time with her and William, showing them love and attention. It was an awful mismatch right from the start.

They both struggled on, doing their best. When William was nine months old, the Prince and Princess made an official visit to Australia and New Zealand. Diana insisted on bringing her young son along, as she couldn't bear to be separated from him for the lengthy six-week tour. She brought her hand-picked nanny Barbara Barnes who looked after William at a remote farm while his parents zigzagged across the two countries, checking in on him occasionally. They were always met by record crowds who went wild for Diana.

The Princess's first official visit overseas on her own was in September 1982, when she represented The Queen at the State funeral of Princess Grace of Monaco. The Princess's first solo overseas tour was in February 1984, when she travelled to Norway to attend a performance of Carmen by the London City Ballet, of which she was Patron.

Other official overseas visits undertaken with the Prince included Australia (for the bicentenary celebrations in 1988), Brazil, India, Canada, Nigeria, Cameroon, Indonesia, Spain, Italy, France, Portugal and Japan (for the enthronement of Emperor Akihito). Their last joint overseas visit was to South Korea in 1992.

The Princess subsequently visited many countries alone including Germany, the United States, Pakistan, Switzerland, Hungary, Egypt, Belgium, France, South Africa, Zimbabwe and Nepal.

Even though she was still fighting bulimia, a struggling marriage and tension about her husband's sustained relationship with Camilla, Diana got pregnant again in 1984. Diana has often referred to the time before Harry's birth as the happiest in her marriage – with the growing family of three being at peace and content.

Henry Charles Albert David (always known as Harry) was born at 4:20 p.m. on September 15, 1984, weighing in at 6 lb, 14 oz. Diana had known through an ultrasound that he was a boy, but hadn't told Charles, who was disappointed that it wasn't a girl. He commented on this and Harry's red hair – remarks that devastated his wife. She later claimed this was the end of the marriage, and she felt closed off after the birth. Diana had provided the "heir and the spare" and it is unlikely that the Prince and Princess were ever intimate again after Harry's birth.

Despite (or because of) her troubled marriage, Diana started to come into her own on the world stage. She blossomed from a naïve young girl, who was a bit plump with mousy brown hair and the inclination to hunch down to avoid attention, to a confident, stylish and beautiful young woman. She cultivated relationships with many fashion designers – British and otherwise – and began to use fashion as a statement when she was out in the world.

Diana had an almost uncanny sense for how her clothing might enhance her physical presence by what she called her "caring wardrobe." She liked to wear bright and colorful clothes to convey approachability and warmth. She didn't wear gloves (royal shocker) because she liked to touch people and hold their hands. She stopped wearing hats (except for formal occasions) to be more casual and enable hugs and child-cuddling without knocking well-wishers with hat brims.

If the Princess was visiting a hospital for the blind, she would often wear velvet so that she would feel warm and tactile to the patients who couldn't see her.

With her tall and lithe 5'10" frame and casual elegance, she was a fashion designer's dream. She evolved from frills and bows to a sleeker look – thanks to favorite designers like Catherine Walker, Victor Edelstein and Versace who all clamored to dress her.

Her confidence in her appearance is really what made Diana iconic with her wardrobe. She was chic and elegant for any occasion – be it during a hospital visit, overseas state dinner, lunch with a girlfriend or watching videos at home with her boys.

Even her fashion sense with William and Harry bucked the royal system. She dressed them in jeans and tee-shirts for casual days – a far cry from the smocked shirts and short trousers of Charles' childhood. I find it quite interesting that Duchess Kate dresses her children in a rather old-fashioned way – quite different to her late mother-in-law's style. I think she does this so that in public, her children look timeless and classic in photographs. I'm sure in private they are dressed much more modern.

Diana had a current approach to parenting as well. She breastfed her babies for a short time (a royal no-no) and was hands-on with their care, feeding and bathing. In fact, she had a difficult time with nannies – she was firm about how the boys should be treated and disciplined. She fired several nannies that got too close to her sons. They were let go when they couldn't accept that Diana was firmly in charge and not them, as was royal custom.

At the same time, the Princess of Wales believed strongly in the monarchy, and respected the institution into which her children had been born, and in which her son William would one day be King. She insisted upon impeccable manners for her children, and had a high regard for duty and tradition. She also she wanted her boys to have fun, and consistently strove to create as normal a childhood as possible for William and Harry. They went to a pre-school outside of the palace, and Diana took them to McDonald's, local shopping and amusement parks. She even made them wait in line with everyone else.

Diana wanted her boys to appreciate their privileged positions in life and give back to others in need. She spent many hours explaining her charity work, important causes, and the value of simply hugging people and connecting with them. As they grew older, she took them with her on secret visits to hospices and homeless shelters to meet and help the sick, dying and neediest people in society. I'm sure that this training has contributed a large part to the ongoing commitment that both William and Harry have to the public and important causes – particularly mental illness.

William was particularly compassionate to others, and it made Diana immensely proud. He cared about those less favoured, and was kind to everyone – staff, members of the public or his royal relatives. Even though he was only nine years old, Diana found herself confiding in him quite often – asking for his advice about what she should wear to an engagement, what events she should give a pass to, and so on. She probably confided too much for his age but had come to rely on him. He was very mature for someone under the age of ten.

"So, darling, I've told you before about the work I've done with some people less privileged – with cancer, drug problems and the homeless. You know that on top of my official charities, I like to visit these poor, sick men and women – and children – to offer my comfort and support. A kind word, a touch can do wonders, William, to put those who are suffering at ease. And you've kept asking to come along. Tonight, we're going to a homeless shelter called The Passage Centre – you've heard me

speak of it before. They don't know we're coming. No one knows we're coming. We're just going to spend time with some people that are staying there because they have nowhere to go. Be kind William, and listen."

"I will, Mummy," her son said quietly.

"And one more thing, William. You may find that some of these men and ladies have a touch of a smell. They might not bathe as much as you do, or they drink things that give off an odor. And their clothes and hair might not be as tidy as what you're used to. You must ignore this, William, and just look them in the eyes and smile. You must never make them feel badly that they are not dressed as nicely as you are."

William's eyes were wide-eyed. What was going to happen next? "Yes, Mummy," he agreed. From Diana, A Spencer in Turmoil.

Above all, Diana wanted to show her sons the unconditional love and support that she herself had always craved. She hugged and kissed them often, and welcomed their school friends for playdates. Diana tried to make their lives fun and as normal as life could be for two princes – one the future King of England!

From KP, Diana and Charles attended all of their London engagements and awaydays – day trips around the UK. This included the usual royal set pieces in the annual calendar:

- Commonwealth Day
- Easter Service
- State Opening of Parliament
- Trooping the Colour (official celebration of the Queen's birthday)
- Royal Ascot
- Chelsea Flower Show
- Order of the Garter Ceremony
- Royal Garden Parties
- Summer Balmoral Break

- Remembrance Day
- Annual Diplomatic Reception
- Christmas and New Year's at Sandringham

For some of these occasions, Charles and Diana would have to wear ceremonial garb – a chance for the Princess to wear a designer evening frock and valuable jewels including tiaras. Many of these jewels belong to the Queen and are loaned out for such events.

Of course, KP was the home base for all the Wales' social events like movie premieres, the opera and ballet, museum events, church and military engagements. They attended weddings, funerals and christenings from their London house. Did you know Prince Charles has twenty-seven godchildren and Diana had seventeen?

Kensington Palace was also the London site for Charles and Diana's parties and events. They hosted state dinners for visiting dignitaries and friends, as well as local and world-famous celebrities. Oprah Winfrey had lunch with Diana at KP, as did the reporter Barbara Walters. The Princess was also known to charm curmudgeonly local press at her famous luncheons.

Physical fitness was a high priority to the Princess – especially after she conquered bulimia. Not only did she want to look good, it was important for her to feel her best. For most of her marriage, she drove to Buckingham Palace on a daily basis for a swim workout. She also jogged and rollerbladed all over Kensington Palace Gardens – usually early or late in the day to avoid being recognized. She had a gym membership at the Chelsea Harbour Club and went for almost-daily workouts – including strength training and tennis with friends. I'm sure this was a great way to relieve the enormous stress she was under – especially as the marriage collapsed.

Diana had a lifelong fascination with alternative therapies, and many practitioners were admitted through the KP gates for consultations and treatments. These included acupuncturists, astrologists, psychics, energy healers, and more traditional massage and reflexology treatments. She and the Duchess of York also regularly received colonic irrigation treatments to remove the toxins from their bodies.

In hindsight, this seems like a desperate plea for help from an unhappy woman. Sadly, some of these practitioners probably told her what she wanted to hear, and assured her that their treatment would be the one to ease her pain and suffering. It's likely some of these treatments even interfered with each other. And I'm pretty certain that the Princess didn't share her long-standing struggle with bulimia to many of these healers. She also suffered from chronic sleeplessness and took sleeping pills on and off for years.

So, between her sons, her royal duties and engagements, overseas tours, exercise, personal treatments, lunch with friends, shopping and so on, Diana lived a frantic life at KP.

To add to this stress, the royal marriage was failing at an alarming pace. Diana's obsession with Charles' friendship with Camilla caused her to question and challenge her husband's every move. They fought constantly, and neither one of them had the communications skills to meet halfway. Diana tended to yell and scream at Charles, which caused him to retreat and withdraw. This pattern settled in early, and eroded the relationship one day at a time.

Around 1986, it's pretty well recorded that Prince Charles resumed his physical affair with Camilla. They had remained close friends throughout the marriage but had kept it platonic. Once they became lovers, the final nail was hammered into the coffin of the Wales' marriage. Charles began to make Highgrove his unofficial headquarters and spent as much time as he could there, barring London engagements and other travel. His long-term love Camilla became his Highgrove hostess for weekend parties and dinner events. Diana effectively took over the Kensington Palace home as her primary residence. Over the next few years, the two saw each other as little as possible, as they continued to keep up the public façade of the "fairy tale marriage."

Diana also found solace outside of the marriage with the ruggedly handsome Major James Hewitt of the Household Cavalry. She asked him to teach her to ride horses to overcome her childhood fear, but this was really just a ruse to get to know him better. The relationship lasted much longer than the riding lessons – about five years off and on. Diana received the love and attention she craved from this attentive and loving officer. He adored the Princess and was always available to her – two things she desperately needed from her husband.

By this time, Diana was pretty much addicted to the telephone. She spent hours each day talking to friends, family, therapists, and other supporters. Once cell phones were available, she often carried two or three so she could continue long conversations when phone batteries ran out. She craved validation, and sought multiple opinions when making decisions. She often didn't take much of this advice, but she needed to talk things out – often for hours at a time.

Although busy with his career, James was able to speak to Diana when she needed him, and the two spent a lot of physical time together as well. He was smuggled into KP in the trunk of a car, and spent many weekends at Highgrove with Diana and the boys when Charles was away. He grew close to William and Harry who idolized the military man. He had miniature fatigues made to measure for the princes who spent hours pretending to be army soldiers.

Diana also travelled to Devon with Hewitt and her PPOs to spend relaxed weekends with his mother at her cottage. Diana's desire to live a normal life was played out in these weekend getaways. She reportedly helped wash dishes and tidy up. She was never much of a cook but may have made an occasional salad.

Her affair with Hewitt fizzled out after he had returned from active duty in the Gulf War in 1991. She may have realized there was no future in the relationship – how could she possibly be an army wife? She probably also tired of him – he was charming and handsome, but may not have shared Diana's passions and interests. In any case, the relationship ended.

James Hewitt then earned the title the "Love Rat" with his tell-all memoir about his affair with Diana called *Princess in Love.* It's a rather sappy view of their relationship, and crossed the royal line by opening the curtain into the life of a senior royal. Diana was humiliated and livid over the betrayal.

Diana's name was also linked to James Gilbey, Oliver Hoare and Will Carling. In my personal opinion, I don't think she had physical relationships with all these men, but continued her lifelong search for acceptance, validation and love from attentive and successful men. She was also flirtatious, which added to her reputation of multiple affairs.

There was a tremendous scandal surrounding Diana's affair with Oliver Hoare. He was an Egyptian art dealer who was actually friends with Prince Charles. And he was married.

Tellingly, Diana began her affair with Hoare soon after her father died. The 7th Earl Spencer had been in hospital with pneumonia, but expected to recuperate. So, it was a shock and surprise when Diana was notified of her father's death while on a Swiss skiing trip with Charles and the children. She loved her father dearly and was heartbroken to hear of his passing.

Where the hell was Raine anyway? For someone who was so glued to Daddy's side, she couldn't have been there to hold his hand? Diana knew she was being unfair, but too overcome with grief to care. She'd lost her beloved Daddy, one of her staunchest supporters over the years.

"I think the doctors had told her Daddy was going to be all right, so she went back to Althorp to deal with some estate business. I haven't spoken to her but I understand she's on her way back. I'm meeting Jane at the hospital shortly. When will you return?" Sarah was trying to focus on the immediate details and necessary arrangements.

"It's too late for tonight, but I'm catching the first plane out of here tomorrow. I should arrive by mid-morning but Charles is not coming with me. I can't bear to play happy families – not now. The palace and the press can just go hang themselves." The Princess of Wales was vehement in her decision. From, Diana, A Spencer in Turmoil

Eventually, Diana was persuaded by the Queen herself to return to London with Charles to attend the funeral. It was a sham show of togetherness, but necessary from the palace perspective. They arrived and left separately, but the public still believed the marriage was intact as the Prince showed his loving support to his grieving wife.

Interestingly, Diana made up with her stepmother after the funeral and the two enjoyed a friendship of casual teas and lunches until the Princess's death.

Diana was vulnerable at this time and so didn't use the best judgement in starting up a dalliance with Hoare. His wife learned of the affair and he abruptly broke it off.

Diana reacted badly and proceeded to embark on a series of nuisance calls to his home. She would call him at all times of the day and night, and hang up when someone answered. It was eventually reported to the police and the hundreds of calls were traced to KP or locations nearby. So embarrassing for Diana! She blamed it on a bullying schoolboy but no one bought this explanation.

This episode shows how desperate Diana was for love and attention. She would become infatuated with a man, obsess over him convinced he was "the one," and eventually drive him away with her neediness and demands for 100% devotion.

1992 was also the year that Diana collaborated with Andrew Morton to write and publish the famous biography *Diana, Her True Story.*

Diana really believed that no one understood her side of the story – how unhappy she was in her marriage due to her husband's indifference and love affair with the married Camilla Parker-Bowles, and the lack of support from the Queen and royal family. She knew the press would misinterpret any interviews she gave to set the record straight. She believed a book would be her chance to show how badly she'd been mistreated, and couldn't be misconstrued or warped by the palace or fact-twisting media.

In order to distance herself from the book, Diana used a go-between – an old friend Dr. James Colthurst – to communicate with Morton. He would bring her lists of questions from the author, and Diana would eagerly give her answers. In this way, she could honestly say later that she had never met the author. This process continued for some months. I'm sure Andrew Morton couldn't believe his luck when this bombshell landed in his lap. To say that it was explosive is a massive understatement. Diana also allowed her closest friends to speak to Morton to confirm some of the stories.

I personally believe that before the book was published Diana had serious second thoughts about exposing the royal family so explicitly. She had to have known it would have a major impact on all her relationships with the royals and everyone around them. Her brother -in-law Robert Fellowes was Private Secretary to the Queen – an important position in the royal household. When the book was first published, she vehemently denied any prior knowledge of the book, its contents or the author. He relayed this to his boss, the Queen who also initially believed her daughter-in-law.

The book was an instant global bestseller and was the shocking expose that Diana wanted. At first, the family believed that Diana's friends had betrayed her and were outraged on her behalf. It soon became blatantly obvious that Diana herself was heavily involved in the book, if not having practically written it herself. The voice was hers, the stories were hers, and no one but Diana knew so many of the insider details. Sympathy turned to fury.

No one was angrier and more humiliated than Charles. Although he had heard rumors of a book, he probably didn't believe that his wife would go so far as to actually see it through – have it written and published.

Before the book release, excerpts were serialized in the Sunday Times. The first headline was stunning and gasp-inducing: "Diana Driven to Five Suicide Bids By Uncaring Charles." It was far worse than Charles could ever have imagined.

"Diana, I don't know what you think you're playing at, but this is abominable. You're making a laughingstock of me, our marriage and the monarchy. What the hell do you think you're doing?" His voice was deathly quiet but menacing.

"*Charles, I don't know what you're talking about. I'm as surprised as you about this story. I don't know who has been ratting to the papers.*" She tried a convincing tone but it sounded hollow even to her own ears. Her blush gave away her bluster.

"*I may be foolish Diana, but I'm not a bloody idiot. This has your fingerprints all over it. What am I supposed to tell my mother? What are you trying to accomplish?*"

Diana began to cry again. "*I swear I've never even met this Andrew Morton character, Charles. As usual, you don't believe anything I tell you. And maybe you should tell your mother that the reason your wife has come to this point is because of you and your lifelong affair with that woman. How about that?*" She was shrieking at her husband as they both glared at but did not touch each other.

"*Stop it, Diana. Your tears lost the ability to move me years ago. Turn them off.*" *He sounded weary.* From Diana, A Spencer in Turmoil.

Charles and Diana had discussed separation before – both were desperate for a way out but couldn't imagine how to part ways. Neither one of them believed it was the right thing to have a separated or divorced Prince and Princess of Wales. The memory of the scandal of Charles' great-uncle David's abdication was still an open wound in the royal family, and neither Charles or Diana wanted to bring further dishonor to the Windsors with their own tawdry issues.

It also cannot be stressed strongly enough that Diana never wanted her boys to go through what she did with divorced parents, coming from a broken home and living between two parents' homes. I think marrying Charles as the Princess of Wales and eventual Queen Consort had given Diana a sense of security that she believed to be unshakeable.

When the Prince and Princess met with the Queen, she counselled time and patience. She was appalled to think of a divorced heir to the throne. Her Majesty had refused her sister's marriage to a divorced man in 1955, which had broken Margaret's heart. How could she countenance this act for her own son and future monarch?

It's well known that the Queen stays out of her children's personal lives. She is a private person herself; and likely believes she has no business in the marriages of her children. However, she is also supportive and gives practical and thoughtful advice when asked. Throughout the years, both she and the Duke of Edinburgh were caring and sympathetic to Diana and her issues. The Princess certainly confided in "Mama" many times during her marriage. Both the Queen and Duke were seriously troubled over Diana's eating disorder, emotional health and ability to cope with royal life and its harsh public scrutiny. They may not have always known how to help her or their son, but never doubt that they really cared.

After the Morton book was published, the Wales's marriage deteriorated quickly. The *Squidgygate* tapes that came to light in the summer of 1992 just made things worse. At first it was reported that a ham radio operator had accidentally taped a private and sometimes intimate conversation between her and James Gilbey. Terms of endearment were exchanged, with James calling the Princess *Squidgy* multiple times. Diana was quoted saying her life was torture and the family didn't appreciate all she did for them. Later on, it was suspected (but never proven) that it was palace courtiers that had bugged the Princess while she was at Sandringham for Christmas. In fact, Diana knew about the tape for months, if not years, before it was leaked to the press. The whole incident was humiliating for Diana and the royals.

By this point, Charles and Diana were spending as little time together as possible. They could barely stand the sight of each other, and only appeared as a couple or family as a show for their sons, or for immovable royal engagements.

By now, 1992 was already shaping up to be what the Queen later called her "annus horribilis." Princess Anne had separated from Captain Mark Philips, and the Duke and Duchess of York's marriage was also finished. When Windsor Castle suffered a terrible fire, it concluded a horrible year for the House of Windsor.

Under tremendous pressure from Buckingham Palace, Charles and Diana fulfilled one last formal commitment together – an overseas trip to South Korea. Diana resisted going, saying it was a sham and only went under great duress. Neither she or Charles made much of an effort to show a united front for the press and were duly dubbed "The Glums" for their sad and miserable faces when photographed together. It was their last official trip together.

Shortly thereafter, the end was inevitable. In December, it was announced that the Prince and Princess of Wales were separating. It was shocking and sad to many of us. How could this fairy tale be over so soon? The Wales' had only been married for eleven years. What would happen next?

Diana always claimed that the separation was a victory, and all she wanted. She hoped for the freedom she craved and an amicable co-parenting relationship with Charles. Divorce was never an option for her.

The Princess moved her things out of Highgrove as KP became her permanent address. Both Charles and Diana quickly eradicated the presence of each other in their respective primary residences by removing personal items and photographs. Charles kept his office and London base at St. James' Palace while making Highgrove his principal home. He began redecorating his Cotswold estate immediately, bringing back a more classic and heavy style to the furnishings and décor.

Barely had 1993 begun when yet another scandal broke – this one surrounding the Prince and his love, Camilla Parker-Bowles. *Camillagate* was even more damaging than *Squidgygate* had been the previous summer. Here was another leaked tape showing an incredibly intimate conversation between Charles and his long-term mistress. Reading the transcript or listening to the tape, you'll be in no doubt of the deep feelings these two have for each other. It's a lengthy conversation filled with endearments, the casual comfort of a long-term relationship and a yearning wistfulness to be together again. There's also some graphic material that is beyond shocking, especially from the Prince of Wales!

The public reception to the tape ranged from horror to disgust, but since Charles and Diana were already separated, it merely added to the general public resentment against the future King, and greatly boosted the Princess's popularity.

As the Prince and Princess started their lives apart, they each settled into new routines, including the pursuit of personal passion causes. William and Harry started spending individual time with each parent, a reality that Diana never wanted. She resented the fact that Charles hired Tiggy Legge-Bourke as a part-time nanny and companion for the boys. Tiggy was the sporty daughter of an aristocrat, and well-loved by the princes. Diana grudged the time that Tiggy spent with "her babies" as the nanny called William and Harry, and this caused grief and bitterness.

In one of her less-than-finer moments, Diana even approached Tiggy at a party and made a snide comment insinuating that the nanny had lost the Prince of Wales's baby – a completely unfounded accusation. Tiggy then sued the Princess but the matter was settled out of court.

Diana's loneliness certainly became more acute at this time. She had always called KP her "gilded cage" – both a respite and a prison, but now with only seeing her sons half the time, it became an even more gloomy place.

She was always an incredibly busy person and continued to fill her time with her sons and school activities (always her number one priority), official engagements, her many friends, fitness and various therapies and alternative treatments. She also made appearances at several royal occasions like *Trooping the Colour*, but joyfully abandoned family holidays at Balmoral and Sandringham.

Throughout her life, Diana embraced and shed many friendships. She had a tendency to get close to people at certain times, then later take offence at some slight, find them disloyal and freeze them out. This is fairly typical of how royals end relationships. All of a sudden, calls are not returned, dates are broken and a close friend is left questioning what he or she may have done wrong to raise the royal ire.

Royals have the luxury of having someone else do their dirty work for them. Staff potty-train dogs, senior staff fire junior workers, and private secretaries or ladies-in-waiting remove unwanted attentions from grasping hangers-on or pushy friends.

Over the years, Diana was no different. She always had a wide circle of friends, but the players constantly changed. She was a demanding friend, and once mobile phones came into play would spend hours endlessly discussing her troubles with those close to her. They needed to be available on demand and 100% supportive of the Princess.

She also kept her friendships separate. She would meet for lunches or dinners, have a tennis match, or attend the cinema with just one or two friends. She was deeply suspicious of friends talking to the press or revealing her secrets, so kept these friendships in different compartments. When she started dating after the separation, some of her friends knew every detail of the budding romances; others were kept completely in the dark. The only friend she kept consistently throughout her life was Carolyn Bartholomew – her old Coleherne Court flat mate. Diana was even godmother to Carolyn's son Jack.

Diana had her famous friends as well: Elton John, Gianni Versace, Oprah Winfrey, Michael Jackson and other celebrities who wanted to be part of the royal circle. Many of them (and others that we'll never know about) were invited to private lunches or dinners with the Princess at KP. Diana treasured her personal relationship with Mother Teresa, who she met on several occasions. Sadly, they both died within a week of each other. Diana was buried with a rosary that Mother Teresa had given her; a prized possession.

Diana also had a renowned friendship with her sister-in-law Sarah Ferguson, the Duchess of York. The two had met before Diana married Charles, and Sarah was one of the few visitors that the new fiancé lunched with during her six-month stay at Buckingham Palace. Diana set up her new friend Sarah with her brother-in-law Prince Andrew and the two hit it off right away.

The newest royal brides were good friends for many years. They bonded over struggling to fit in, learning the royal life, and being young Mums together. They were a tremendous support to each other over lengthy family holidays in Scotland as their respective marriages crumbled. They joked together and called themselves the Wicked Wives of Windsor.

At one point, Diana and Sarah even made a pact to leave the royal family together. Sarah was the first to jump in early 1992, and Diana watched eagerly (and with growing horror) to see what would happen to the Duchess. Regrettably, Sarah was axed cleanly out of the Windsor dynasty almost immediately, and this frightened the Princess to imagine how she would be treated outside the palace walls.

The pair had an on-again, off-again relationship throughout the years. Diana loved her sister-in-law, but felt she made bad choices at times. The Princess of Wales always held herself to a high standard, especially in public.

The final breach between the two friends came when Sarah wrote her autobiography *My Story* – a royal no-no by all accounts. In it, she accused Diana of borrowing a pair of shoes from her and then giving the Duchess a wart. Diana was incensed by this – and the fact that Fergie kept bringing up her famous sister-in-law in her press interviews. The Princess froze out Sarah and never reconciled with her, despite repeated attempts by Fergie to apologize and make amends. Sadly, Diana probably also lost touch with her beloved nieces Beatrice and Eugenie.

"If she wants to write a sordid little story of her royal life, that's her right, I suppose." Diana shrugged. "But slagging me and then doing nothing but speak of me in all her interviews – especially in America - is just too much. I used to feel sorry for poor Fergie but not anymore. She's cooked her own goose."

Paul nodded sympathetically, knowing his boss was immovable on this subject. Sarah had been ringing, writing letters and even showing up at the KP gates unannounced in a despairing attempt to reconcile with her ex sister-in-law. But to no avail. Paul had tried to comfort the hysterical Duchess who wanted her old chum back. He really hoped that with time, Diana would relent and end the freeze-out as she had with others. The two had been the greatest of friends throughout their years as the Wicked Wives of Windsor, and Paul himself had a soft spot for the once-cheerful redhead. Only time would tell, he thought to himself. From Diana, A Spencer Forever

Paradoxically, Diana was well-renowned for never forgetting a birthday or special occasion for the people she cared about. She routinely shopped Kensington High Street for distinctive gifts for her seventeen godchildren, numerous friends, and even staff members and their families. She also kept in touch with many people she met at hospitals, hospices or special events. Once she made a connection with someone, she would maintain it for life. This was all done quietly in the background.

At this time, Diana also made a special friend in an unusual place – the press. The Princess was well known for alerting the media to specific events where she wanted to be photographed, or the attention drawn to her rather than Charles. She personally placed stories now and then to ensure her side of a particular story was spread. She befriended Richard Kay from *The Daily Mail* and the two lunched together from time-to-time. He was sympathetic to Diana's story which he reflected in his reporting. Richard was one of the last people to speak to her on the final day of her life.

Someone else who was privy to the Princess's confidences was her son William. Diana was close to both her sons, but was especially close to her eldest who also happens to be a future King of England. As a parent,

Diana magnificently balanced her loving guidance towards duty and responsibility, with creating a fun and ordinary life for both her sons.

Diana was always open with both William and Harry about many aspects of life – including taking them on secret visits to the homeless and desperately ill. Diana was affectionate with the princes, and encouraged them to talk about their emotions and feelings. It's remarkable that Diana was able to break the cycle of her own lack of childhood emotional support by providing a healthy and warm environment for her own children.

The Princess often asked William for advice. This could include anything from what to wear to a movie opening to what charities to be involved with. It also included his guidance about how to handle issues and problems. Diana was known to have said that William was wise beyond his years.

Without doubt, Diana confided to some degree in her son about her troubled relationship with his father. We'll never know to what extent this happened, but at the time of the separation William was only ten years old. I'm afraid that Diana may have overshared with her son, and told him things he probably couldn't handle. Separation and divorce are extremely difficult for children, and they shouldn't be placed in the middle of their parents' issues. I'm sure William was empathetic and supportive to his mother, but I hope she didn't put him in an impossible position. Both boys admired and still love both their mother and father.

As a rich, famous, beautiful and available young Princess, Diana was in great demand. She had many friends but dated very little. She dipped her toes in the romance pool slowly after her separation. She was conscious that the public eye was on her, and as the mother of a future King, she couldn't put a foot wrong. Nor she did want to jeopardize any access to her sons.

She tended to go for similar types: well-to-do charming and sophisticated men from good backgrounds and upper-class families. And of course, tall and handsome!

She was linked to a rugby player named Will Carling but this was never proven or acknowledged by the Princess.

As Charles and Diana settled into an easier time separated than married, the acrimony slowed down, and the two co-parented William and Harry in an amicable way. They both continued with their busy schedules of engagements, trips and royal commitments.

All of this changed in June of 1994 when Prince Charles gave his famous television interview. Ostensibly, the interview was a companion piece to Jonathon Dimbleby's biography to commemorate his 25th investiture anniversary as Prince of Wales. Charles spoke for over two hours about his philanthropy, his role within the Royal Family, and his views on religion, policy and Britain's future. It was really an attempt to elevate his stature and good works while showing he had the capacity and competence to become a good monarch.

However, most people only remember two minutes of the interview when the Prince admitted to cheating on his wife, and maintaining a relationship with Camilla. It was Charles' attempt to set the record straight, but it backfired in a spectacular way. Public support had always been in Diana's camp and this just increased it tenfold.

I'm sure Diana herself was deeply hurt and distressed by this televised admission. I believe she still loved Charles and would have reconciled with him if she thought he could have changed and given up Camilla. But of course, he couldn't.

On the night that the interview aired, the Princess rallied and went to a scheduled engagement at the Serpentine Gallery. She wore what became known as the revenge dress – a black, off-the-shoulder, fitted and becoming Christina Stambolian original that knocked Prince Charles off the front pages the next day. His public relations attempt failed miserably, and the Prince continued to be seen as a cold and uncaring husband and father. This was an unfair label and proven wrong over time, but Charles didn't help himself with this interview and shocking admission.

Although she didn't retaliate right away, Diana's anger simmered, along with her own desire to set the record straight. She asked a number of her friends and advisors if she should tell her side of the story in a television interview. Horrified, they all advised against it. But Diana didn't listen.

On November 20, 1995, Diana sat down with Martin Bashir for the BBC program *Panorama* for an astonishing interview. A staggering 22.8 million people watched it, and it remains one of the highest-rated BBC programs of all time.

The Princess had chosen Bashir due to his gentle and sympathetic style. She had reviewed the questions in advance and rehearsed her answers to present herself as calm and in control. She told no one of the interview in advance; not the Queen nor Charles nor any of her staff including her Private Secretary Patrick Jephson.

Diana dropped bombshell after bombshell including:

- She had an affair with James Hewitt and had been in love with him.
- She knew about Camilla and struggled because there were "three of us in the marriage and it was a bit crowded."
- The ongoing affair caused her rampant bulimia.

- She struggled with post-natal depression and a heartless royal family who didn't understand her.

The most damaging statements Diana made, however, had to do with the fitness of Charles to be King. She expressed concern that he couldn't adapt to or handle the top job. She intimated that she thought the crown should be passed over to their son, William.

Reaction to the devastating interview was swift and decisive. As usual, the public was supportive and loyal. The outpouring of caring and defense of the Princess was overwhelming. Diana received bags of cards and letters from fans sharing their own stories of loveless marriages and affairs. The press was outraged on her behalf.

The response from the palace and those close to Diana was rather different. Charles and the Queen were furious. The Duke of Edinburgh was apoplectic with rage. Even Princess Margaret who had always been one of Diana's biggest supporters wrote her a scathing letter. Diana's brother-in-law Sir Robert Fellowes couldn't believe the Princess had done it again – gone public with a tasteless and flawed tell-all without prior royal approval. And her son William was humiliated and embarrassed by his mother's admission of an extra-marital affair.

Did Diana regret this interview? In hindsight, she probably did. Believing you can manipulate the media is impossible, as others have found before and since. I believe at first, she probably thought the interview went well. She stayed composed, answered calmly and firmly, and hit home her key points.

However, she underestimated the impact on the Queen and royal family. Her Majesty immediately summoned her son and daughter-in-law to Buckingham Palace and demanded divorce proceedings begin at once. This was Diana's worst fear come to life. She had steadfastly maintained that she never wanted a divorce, and that she and Charles could co-exist forever as separated co-parents within the royal machine. She also thought that she could someday be Queen or some sort of role as Queen Consort.

The *Panorama* interview firmly closed the door on any of these options. The Queen and Duke were not going to allow Diana any more opportunities to air dirty laundry in public. They had to take control of the situation.

After she returned to London, Diana was summoned to Buckingham Palace to meet with the Queen and Prince Charles. Although nervous, Diana was grateful for the opportunity to present her own case to the monarch and her husband directly. Prince Philip was not in attendance.

After the formalities had been attended to, the Queen got to the matter-at-hand.

"Charles, Diana. I've called you here today to urge you in the strongest terms to proceed with the divorce at once. The Duke and I are saddened that the situation has come to this, but it has and it's time to finalize the divorce. It's in the best interests of everyone, especially the boys" Her Majesty, Queen Elizabeth II made her statements calmly and with an air of finality.

"But, Mama. I don't want a divorce. I still love Charles. None of what's happened is my fault, surely you see that." Diana pleaded with her mother-in-law.

Charles stood by silently, with his hands behind his back. At age forty-eight, the heir to the British throne was still a good-looking man. His hair was greying quite visibly, and he might not have been as lean as he once was, but his piercing blue eyes were as mesmerizing as ever. And although he seemed quite agitated, he still exuded that sense of manliness and courtliness that had always appealed to the Princess. He fidgeted with his cufflinks and said nothing, waiting for his mother to respond.

"Diana, I think discussing or apportioning blame at this point is inconsequential and bears no fruit. You've both done and said some distasteful things – particularly in the public eye – that make it impossible to follow any other course of action."

She gazed in the direction of her son.

"Hmmph," he paused looking towards the fireplace. "I agree with Her Majesty, Diana. Let's end this crisis and proceed with the divorce straightaway. Please don't make this harder than it already is."

"Harder than it is?" repeated Diana incredulously. "Charles, you're the one who couldn't leave his mistress alone for the entire length of our marriage. You don't think that was hard for me?"

"Diana, please," the Prince spread out his arms in a useless gesture. "The time for all that acrimony is over. Please," he repeated. He refused to be drawn into another futile row – especially in front of the Queen of England.

Diana turned to the monarch. "Does this mean Charles will be re-marrying?" she posed in an outraged tone.

The Queen looked straight at her daughter-in-law. "I should think that's very unlikely," she replied quietly.

Diana fought to keep her tears at bay. "I want you both to know that I never wanted a divorce. I thought we had come to terms on how we could all stay in an arrangement that works – for the palace, for us and most especially for William and Harry. An amicable separation with proper roles for Charles and myself. I see now that it's impossible," the Princess acknowledged in defeat.

"Thank you, Diana. I believe what we're all in perfect accord about is to minimize the impact on the boys. You are their mother, and that will never change. You will always be in their lives. You have my word." The Queen quickly summarized the agreement.

"Thank you, Mama," Diana managed to squeak out without bursting into tears.

The Queen rose, signifying the end of the interview. "We'll be sending you papers to finalize arrangements very soon. Again, I must repeat that the Duke and I couldn't be more disappointed to see the union end this way."

The audience had lasted twenty-one minutes." From Diana, A Spencer Forever

Diana was distraught over the royal command, and spent hours on the phone with friends sobbing her heart out. She was deathly afraid of losing her children. After all, the Queen had legal custody of William and Harry until they turned the age of majority. It was always quite unlikely that the sovereign would take over the day-to-day decisions about her grandsons, but she legally had the right.

The Princess of Wales then dried her tears and got to work. She hired British lawyer Anthony Julius, known for his toughness and tenacity. Diana was determined that if this divorce was to go through, she needed to fight for the best possible settlement for herself. Divorce negotiations began and were to continue until mid-1996 when a final settlement was reached.

In late 1995, Diana met the met she called "Mr. Wonderful" and "Drop Dead Gorgeous" – Dr. Hasnat Khan. She had met him by chance at the Royal Brompton Hospital when she was visiting the husband of her friend and acupuncturist Oonagh Toffolo who was being treated by Dr. Khan. The first meeting had more of an impact on Diana than the doctor, who barely noticed the Princess. She was immediately smitten.

After two weeks of daily visits, Diana and Hasnat started to connect and date. To look at them as a couple, they would seem ill-matched. Diana was young, royal, glamorous, rich, fit and worldly. Hasnat was a Muslim heart surgeon from Pakistan who worked 90-hour work weeks, was intensively private; and smoked and dined on Guinness and fried chicken. But they also had a lot in common – they were both passionate about helping the sick and disadvantaged, and were tireless in this pursuit.

Diana loved Hasnat's brown eyes and compassionate nature. Hasnat fell in love with Diana's charm, beauty and kind-heartedness.

Over the next two years, the pair carried on a clandestine relationship, mostly over dinners at KP. As with others, Hasnat was smuggled into the palace under a blanket in the back seat or the trunk of the car, often picked up by Paul Burrell, Diana's butler. I can only imagine how humiliating this was!

Diana would also sneak over to Hasnat's Chelsea flat which was the furthest thing from a bachelor pad. Given his long hours at the hospital, Hasnat's home was just a place to sleep, grab a quick shower and fast food, and race back to the hospital. Diana allowed her nesting instincts an outlet by tidying up his flat while she waited for him – washing his dishes, cleaning the floor, dusting, straightening and even ironing for her lover.

As the relationship progressed, Diana and Hasnat would go out to a jazz club for drinks or dinner once in a while. In order to avoid recognition, Diana would wear a long wig and glasses. I'm sure she took great delight in deceiving the public and ever-present paparazzi.

Five hours later, Hasnat returned to his spotless flat. Greeting him was a tall, beautiful blonde wearing a full-length white faux fur coat and a smile. And nothing else. Diana greeted her lover with a long and lingering kiss. It was quite some time before the two dressed; and with Diana in her disguise, ate fish and chips at the local chipper.

They returned to the flat much later and snuggled up together on the sofa, with the Princess chattering all the while, and Hasnat doing his utmost to keep up with her.

"Tell me more about the local hospitals, Diana. How were they equipped? What manner of injuries were they coping with?" Hasnat had an arm casually draped over Diana's shoulder.

"They had almost nothing, Natty." Diana shook her head in dismay. *"Tiny little hospitals – rooms really – with beds and people of all sorts. Children, adults – and the babies! All with severe damage from the landmines. Mainly, legs and arms blown off. Sometimes both legs - they were bedridden, hoping some day for prosthetics so they might walk again. The doctors had that rather glazed look in their eyes from lack of sleep, not enough medications and supplies, and well, lack of everything, I suppose. It was all very somber and depressing. And the heat too. It was overwhelming, Natty."*

"So, what are the doctors doing for their patients?" pressed the doctor, eager to understand the facts of the situation.

"Mainly just trying to keep them alive, darling. In some cases, amputation. In others, just waiting for them to die. Some would go home after their wounds had healed but to what? A life with no hands? How could a man work or provide for his family? I saw very little in the way of medicines. Everything seemed to be in short supply. The Red Cross brought some well-needed pain medications, but it hardly seemed enough. They are heroes, those doctors. And nurses." Diana's eyes clouded at the memories.

"And you yourself are an angel, my dear," smiled Hasnat as he gazed into Diana's eyes. *"To go all that way to offer your support and caring – with such personal sacrifice and risk. I admire you greatly, Diana."*

She preened at the compliment. Natty was rather introverted, even when he wasn't distracted with his work. So, any small words of praise were soaked in like golden rays of sunlight on a dark day. *"That means so much to me, Natty. I don't know what it is. I just feel so compelled to help each and every person. To look beyond the wounds, the blood, the smell of death, and see the humanity lying on the bed. It seems hopeless at times and that just a touch or hug doesn't matter. But I know it does. For even a few minutes, they are taken out of their pain. I try to joke with them, give them a kind word, hug them. It's all I have to give but I'll keep offering it until someone stops me. There is so much need in the world. Hasnat, I want to go to Bosnia and find a way to get to Cambodia. I really feel I've found my calling. This is what I'm meant to be doing in this chapter of my life. I won't stop." Diana's voice was alive with passion and purpose. Her blue eyes sparkled.*

"And darling, you will get to Cambodia and Bosnia. And anywhere else you set your mind to. I have such faith in you. I think you really can change the world – one person at a time." Hasnat gave her a tender kiss.

"Somehow, we must find a way to work together, Natty," the Princess continued eagerly. "With your talent as a doctor and connections – and my drive and ability to marshal resources almost anywhere – we should start our own hospital. Or mobile caring centre. Or something. Just think of what we could do together!" Diana's eyes were shining at the possibilities. To be able to live and work with the man she loved – it was all she had ever wanted. From Diana, A Spencer Forever

Hasnat and the Princess carried on this clandestine romance for two years, stealing an hour or two when their busy schedules permitted. I'm sure Diana wanted more of Hasnat's time than he was able to give her, but she certainly understood his important commitments. She even took up an interest in medicine, reading medical journals and watching a surgery.

Diana also cultivated a fascination for Muslim and Pakistani culture and tradition. Most people don't know she was a voracious reader and always had a pile of books to be read – and not just romance novels. She would explore alternative philosophies and religions, and other causes that drew her attention. She also reached out to Hasnat's family and even visited them in Pakistan – without her lover's knowledge. While gracious to the Princess, there was never the open-armed affection and acceptance from them that she craved.

The long-term success of this relationship was always doomed. Diana pictured a marriage, a daughter and a happy life supporting her incredible heart surgeon husband. Hasnat wanted no part of royal life, publicity or the pressure of the merciless media. They loved each other but could not see a viable way forward. After some on-again, off-again breakups and reconnections, Hasnat broke it off with Diana for good in the late spring of 1997. The Princess still loved him desperately, and they may have reunited if she hadn't died tragically in August 1997. Friends have said that he truly was the love of Diana's life.

As the divorce negotiations continued, Diana struggled to find a new role for herself. She had given the famous "Time and Space speech" in 1993, resigning from over 100 charities of which she was patron. She was looking for a new focus, away from fashion and the traditional royal commitments. She saw herself as a potential British ambassador, and approached government officials and other high-powered connections like Sir Richard Attenborough to try and craft a role for herself in an official capacity. She was stonewalled by the palace courtiers and mainstream politicians. They found her unpredictable and unqualified for a British diplomatic position. This frustrated the Princess who wanted to use her vast popularity and reach beyond England.

The answer finally came to Diana via an unlikely source, her healer Simone Simmons, who alerted her to the world-wide landmine issue. Once she heard about the damage being done to civilians in war-torn countries by undetonated landmines, she was compelled to help. Hearing of innocent men, women and children left limbless even killed by stray landmines broke her heart, and she was determined to help. The Red Cross was delighted to have someone of the Princess's stature and profile associated with this struggling cause.

As with any matter that captured Diana's attention, she wanted to dive in quickly and learn all about it. She took Red Cross briefings and read up on the issues. But what she needed most was to tour the damage for herself firsthand, to see and comfort the victims, and discover how she could help on the ground. She really wanted to go to Cambodia where the need was the greatest, but the Foreign Office refused, citing safety and security issues.

While Diana waited to find an official role, the divorce was being finalized. Dialogue between both sides were unbending. Diana wanted 50% access to the boys and a major say in their upbringing, Kensington Palace as her sole residence and an office at St. James Palace. She also asked for a country estate, a large lump sum payment and an annual allowance. Charles would continue to pay all of William and Harry's expenses including school fees, travel and clothing. Eventually Diana conceded the country property and office space.

The final settlement gave Diana 17 million pounds and everything else that she asked for. She had her press secretary issue a statement outlining the settlement including that she would now be known as Diana, Princess of Wales. The palace was furious at this premature proclamation of the settlement details, and issued a contravening statement saying the specifics were not yet resolved.

The issue of Princess Diana's HRH status has been widely discussed and disputed. Her Royal Highness is an important honorific and conferred on very few people. According to letters patent issued by King George V in 1917, the sons and daughters of sovereigns and the male-line grandchildren of sovereigns are entitled to the style. Those marrying into the royal family or other relatives get this conferred on them by choice of the monarch.

Many have reported that Prince Charles wanted the

HRH title taken away from his soon-to-be ex-wife, but I don't find that consistent with his personality. He's just not that petty. Nor do I consider it something Her Majesty would pursue. It's possible that they were both so exasperated with Diana and her actions over the years that they wanted to punish her in this way, but I don't really believe that. Especially for the mother of a future King.

I think that Diana herself offered to give up her title – perhaps in exchange for getting the assurances of child custody that she wanted. Or she may have suggested she'd be willing to give it up in an impetuous haste or to gain public sympathy, and then regretted it. We'll never know for sure, but we do know that William comforted his mother that he would return the title to her when he became King.

The decree nisi was granted in August 1996. A non-disclosure agreement prohibited either side from sharing the details. The fairy tale romance was finally over. The Prince and Princess of Wales were divorced.

The day after her divorce, Diana announced her resignation from over 100 charities and retained patronages of only six: *Centrepoint, English National Ballet, Great Ormond Street Hospital, The Leprosy Mission, National AIDS Trust* and the *Royal Marsden Hospital*. She continued her work with the *British Red Cross Anti-Personnel Land Mines Campaign,* but was no longer listed as patron.

This would have been a devastating blow to these charities who relied not only on the Princess's personal support but also the cache of her name being associated with their good works. This alone would guarantee them generous donations and broad-based awareness and interest.

Some have reported that Diana resigned these organizations in a fit of pique – a strong message that if the royal family was done with her, she was finished donating so much of her time and energy to their good causes. I think she was extremely hurt and may have acted in haste. It was a lose-lose but the Princess was adamant. She was determined on a fresh start.

Since Diana was unsuccessful in obtaining a country property for herself, she started looking around for a place outside of London where she could take the boys that could compete with Balmoral holidays. Her brother, the 8th Earl Spencer offered her the use of the Garden House on the Althorp Estate. Diana thought it was perfect – her own home on the family estate and a two-hour commute from KP in London. She excitedly started planning, even getting her old friend Dudley Poplak to start remodeling plans.

A few weeks later, Charles Spencer changed his mind and retracted the offer. After much consideration, he decided that the security and safety issues of having the Princess of Wales and her sons on his land were insurmountable. And he didn't want the pressure of the omnipresent photographers, press and curious public to disrupt everyday life.

The Earl's sister was inconsolable. She had her heart set on the Garden House, and bitterly resented Charles going back on his word. He made offers of other properties and houses, but Diana refused them all. She wrote her brother nasty letters that he returned unopened. Sadly, the two were not on speaking terms at the time of her death.

Around this time, Diana credits her son William with giving her the idea to sell off her old gowns for charity. She had wardrobes full of evening dresses and formal gowns that she never wore anymore.

Diana's style had evolved dramatically from the early '80's. She now embraced a sleeker look, leaving behind the frills, poofs and more girlish fashion choices of her early twenties. And I'm sure that not only did she want to discard the out-of-date dresses, she wanted to forget some of the memories they evoked. Whether from happier times, or more stressful ones, she was ready to shed her old life on all levels.

With the help of William and most of her friends, she chose 79 dresses to sell over the next few months. Christie's in New York handled the auction, with the 3.25 million-dollar proceeds going to AIDs and cancer charities. No one in the royal family had ever considered such an action – another example of Diana deciding to go her own way – despite the fallout. Most certainly, the Queen and senior palace officials were probably shocked and scandalized by this unorthodox and public decision. I doubt Diana ever regretted it.

Suddenly William clapped his hands. "Mummy, I have a brilliant idea. Why don't you take all your gowns – especially all the old poofy ones that you never wear anymore – and auction them off for charity? That will make people sit up and notice. Just think how much money you could raise – for AIDS, the homeless, even the Red Cross!" The fourteen-year old Prince was delighted with his own suggestion.

"Are you serious, William? Sell off my wardrobe?" Diana asked slowly.

"Not your entire wardrobe, Mum. Just your ballgowns. You know – the fancy ones that you hardly ever wear? How many do you have? Don't you have a whole roomful of them?"

Diana started to get excited. "You're right, darling. I do have heaps of gruesome old dresses. I would never put most of them on again. Why not sell them for charity? William, you are brilliant." She resisted the urge to hug her son but bestowed her luminous smile upon him. "Paul, Paul," she called excitedly.

The butler came running quickly to aid his mistress.

Yes, Ma'am. Is everything alright?" he asked with concern.

"Yes, yes, Paul, everything is more than alright. William has had a wonderful idea. To auction off my old gowns for charity. Isn't that splendid?" Diana jumped to her feet.

Paul called upon his royal training to retain his reserve.

"Yes, Ma'am. That does seem a marvelous concept. How may I be of assistance?"

"Come on William, Paul, let's have a look at the gowns and start choosing some for the auction." She grabbed her son's hand and ran into the first-floor wardrobe room. Paul strode hard to keep up with the Princess. From Diana, A Spencer Forever

Diana also got some good news about her quest to dive into the landmine issue. She finally got permission from the Foreign Office for a Red Cross-sponsored humanitarian trip to Angola in January 1997. Working with Sir David Attenborough, she took a camera crew with her to make the documentary *The Heart of the Matter* to draw attention to the global landmine issue. She visited and held as many amputees as she could, beaming a light on this issue in the shadows. As the patron of *Halo Trust* that clears debris and landmines, the Princess drew the world's attention with a walk through an Angolan minefield in a ballistic helmet and flak jacket. Of course, the image was splashed on the front pages of the newspapers across the world and is one of the enduring photos of the Princess of Wales.

She was accused of meddling in politics and even called a "loose cannon" by London officials. Despite the criticism, Halo has claimed that Diana's efforts resulted in raising international awareness about landmines and the subsequent sufferings caused by them. In June 1997, she gave a speech about landmines and even travelled to Washington D.C to promote the American Red Cross landmines campaign. She made a follow-up visit to Bosnia and Herzegovina with the Landmine Survivors Network in August, days before her death.

Although these efforts were lost in the tragedy of Diana's death, her work with anti-personnel landmines is truly one of her lasting legacies. A few months after her death in 1997, the International Campaign to Ban Landmines won the Nobel Peace Prize. This is in no small part due to Diana's leadership over this forgotten issue. In 2019, her son Prince Harry visited Angola on an official royal tour and repeated his mother's famous Halo walk. He also spoke to Sandra, the landmine victim whose photo was seen around the world – the amputee who sat on Diana's lap is now a mother of four.

Diana's last summer at Kensington Palace turned out to be a lot busier than she had ever imagined. With the flurry of activity around the Christie's auction, and Diana's trip to Angola, she hadn't planned beyond June. She knew the boys would be spending the month of August and until school started at Balmoral – an annual summer holiday that William and Harry eagerly anticipated.

Diana knew that a hot July around London and Kensington Palace wouldn't cut it for the active young princes. She inquired for options among friends who willingly offered holiday properties in and outside the U.K. Diana was touched but none of the recommendations could be supported with the necessary safety and security measures for the most famous woman in the world and the future King of England.

At a charity dinner, Diana was re-introduced to Mohamed Al-Fayed, the controversial billionaire Egyptian. They had met years earlier, and easily struck up a conversation about summer plans. Al-Fayed quickly offered the use of his St. Tropez villa and private yacht for a summer break for Diana and the boys. It sounded enticing to the Princess, especially when Al-Fayed reassured her that her safety and protection would be of the utmost priority given his own extensive security team.

Al-Fayed had launched a successful shipping company and subsequently became involved in many businesses with his brothers. In the mid-80's he had purchased Harrod's, the signature high-end English department store. He owned the extravagant Hotel Ritz in Paris, along with many elegant residences around the world. At best his reputation was mixed. He ingratiated himself with the aristocracy and royalty of British high society, with limited success. He repeatedly tried and failed to obtain a British passport.

Diana eagerly accepted the offer for a ten-day get-away with Al-Fayed and his family. She knew the billionaire could offer her and the princes the protection they needed, along with a luxury vacation. And the palace agreed! She couldn't wait to spend time with the large Al-Fayed family aboard Mohamed's newly purchased luxury yacht, the *Jonikal*.

Castel Ste. Helene was a four-acre estate within the private community of Les Parc De St Tropez. It boasted a main villa with nine bedrooms, large reception rooms, two kitchens, a children's playroom, swimming pool and terraces. It also housed a waterfront beach house with nine bedrooms, an indoor and outdoor pool, a nightclub with a cinema and a bar, and a gym and sauna. A boathouse, helipad and jetty completed the self-contained compound, which had an impeccable and comprehensive security system.

Diana and the boys stayed in a luxurious four-bedroom guesthouse with a nearby tennis court.

"It's lovely Nora, really lovely. And just what we needed. The boys are having the times of their lives. Jet-skiing, swimming and boating. And you should see the video game console and all the games that Mohamed has. William and Harry think they are in video heaven." Diana was speaking on the telephone to her good friend.

"And how are you getting along with the Al-Fayed family, darling?" asked Nora from a rainy London. "Are they turning on the golden charm?" Nora wasn't as keen for her girlfriend to forge a tight relationship with the notorious Egyptian family, but knew Diana loved the tight-knit middle-eastern family

culture.

"*Golden is right, Nor. It's rather ostentatious, really. Such a break from cold, royal castles. Everything here is warm and open. You know, even the taps in the loo are made of gold! Not to my taste, but marvelous for a holiday. And yes, everything is first-class – the food, drinks and entertainment are always flowing. What I love most, darling, is how the family shows affection for each other. They want to spend time together. It's noisy and messy, and I love it.*"

"*Not quite the same as a holiday at Sandringham*" *joked* Nora.

"*Not even close,*" *snorted Diana. "Or even Althorp for that matter. There's something about this Muslim Asian culture that just speaks to me. I feel welcomed just for myself. Like I'm being wrapped in a warm blanket. Very cozy.*"

"*Very cozy, indeed, Diana. It sounds bloody brilliant. Maybe next time you can bring along your poor London chum.*"

Diana laughed. "I'll do my best, Nor. But wait, let me tell you the best part. Last night, Mohamed's son Dodi joined us at the villa. I've met him before but honestly, didn't really notice him. But he was just as pleasant and amiable as the rest of the family. Really attentive, darling." From Diana, A Spencer Forever.

Soon after Diana and the boys arrived, a surprise visitor made an appearance – Mohamed's son Dodi. We now know that he was nearby on a yacht with his then-girlfriend (or fiancé depending on who you believe) Kelly Fisher. Once the Princess was on board the *Jonikal*, his father quickly summoned him to help amuse Diana and her young sons.

It's been said that it was a little more premeditated on Al-Fayed's part. That he saw an opportunity to match his son with the daughter-in-law of the Queen of England. That he wanted to thumb his nose at the British establishment by inserting himself and his family into the royal family through an unexpected and shocking alliance.

What happened next is a matter of speculation that will never be resolved. Did Dodi and Diana fall madly in love that summer? Were they planning to get married? Was it true that Diana was pregnant? Or was it just a summer romance?

After doing my own research, I'm convinced that it was a short-term fling that went terribly wrong. I believe Diana still had strong feelings for Hasnat Khan, and was smarting from the breakup.

She met Dodi on a beautiful yacht in the Mediterranean under hot and sunny skies. She was having a relaxing time in a warm family environment with her two sons around her. London must have seemed very far away.

Dodi was the perfect antidote to Diana's aching heart. He was tall, dark and handsome. He was rich, sophisticated and charming. And he had nothing but time for the lonely Princess. The two spent hours each day talking, sunbathing and getting to know each other. Dodi was sympathetic and understanding. And they had so much in common – Dodi had lost his mother at a young age, and Diana felt abandoned by her own family.

Dodi's past was a bit sketchy. He was a Hollywood film producer who had worked on the award-winning *Chariots of Fire*. It's rumored he had a drug problem and was unreliable. As the oldest son of Al-Fayed, he led an extravagant lifestyle funded by his father and was known for leaving unpaid bills behind him in his global travels.

At age forty-two Dodi was an international playboy who was known for dating models. He had never married. At the time he met Diana, he was dating American actress Kelly Fisher.

At the beginning of his relationship with Diana, he kept Kelly a secret. He went back and forth between both yachts, until he broke off the relationship with Kelly, as his feelings for Diana deepened.

Kelly claimed the two were engaged and planning a life together in Malibu, California. She was furious with the broken engagement and actually filed a breach of contract lawsuit against him, which was later dropped.

Diana was unaware of most of this until Dodi confessed some version of the truth to her.

She herself wasn't being totally honest with her new lover. I believe she was also sending messages through the media to Hasnat Khan. Both Dodi and Diana looked like they were performing for the cameras that summer. After the first cruise, Diana took the boys back to London where she joined the royal family for the annual Balmoral holiday. Looking at a long lonely summer alone, Diana accepted Dodi's invitation for two more solo trips with him.

The paparazzi found and stalked the new couple. Rather than hiding from the cameras, Dodi and Diana lounged and posed in swimsuits on the yacht's deck. They were even "caught" on camera in an embrace that was dubbed *The Kiss* – a million-dollar photo that circled the globe within twenty-four hours.

Some have claimed the kiss was a set-up, even going so far as to say that Diana tipped off the press as to their location and timing to capture it so a certain Pakistani doctor could see what he was missing. It's hard to know for sure but it wouldn't surprise me. Diana was known to call certain reporters and advise of her plans to ensure a well-timed photo hit the papers at strategic times.

Dr. Khan has never spoken of his two-year relationship with Diana so it can never be confirmed, but it seems likely that he was disturbed at some level to see his former love in the arms of another man.

A sad interruption to Diana's last summer was the July death of Gianni Versace. He was brutally murdered on a walk near his Florida mansion. Diana had grown close to the designer throughout their years-long collaborations and considered him a dear friend. She was devastated by his senseless death.

Diana flew to Italy to be at Elton John's side for the funeral. John was extremely close to Versace and was visibly shaken during the ceremony. Diana laid a hand on his shoulder as he sobbed in grief. This was a bittersweet reunion. The two had not spoken in months after Diana had pulled out from writing a forward to a recent book of Elton's. It's tragic to remember that he re-wrote his *Candle in the Wind* song to sing at Diana's funeral just over a month later.

In August, Diana made a last philanthropic trip to Sarajevo, Bosnia for a three-day visit to draw attention to the fight against landmines. She visited the homes of landmine victims and met with local disability groups and rehabilitation specialists. She was also caught on camera caressing the face of a grieving mother visiting her son's grave at a roadside cemetery. This was a spontaneous act of compassion from a woman who truly cared about others.

Throughout the summer, Dodi was devoted to his new love, calling her when they were apart and sending her extravagant gifts. Diana complained to friends that he was showering her with presents she didn't need or want. I think by mid-August, she was tiring of the romance and finding the immature Dodi a little needy and possessive.

Ironically, the very attributes that had excited Diana about her Egyptian lover were now suffocating her. Both her husband and her latest love Hasnat had been elusive, and didn't give her the undivided attention that she craved. Dodi worked so little that he was available virtually 24/7, which stifled the Princess who lived an extremely busy and diverse life. I highly doubt the relationship would have lasted much beyond the summer if they had both survived the car accident in late August.

As the sunshine and warmth continued, Diana agreed to one last *Jonikal* trip with Dodi before her boys returned from Balmoral and the autumn schedule. She spoke to William and Harry daily, but as always, she missed them terribly when they were with the royal family. She was already planning their reunion and thinking ahead to Harry's 13th birthday on September 15th.

The world interest in Diana and Dodi remained at fever pitch throughout the summer. Their yacht was surrounded by any boats that paparazzi and photographers could hire. Every photo of the duo, no matter how grainy or far away, was instantly published. Dodi started to get frustrated with the constant scrutiny. He'd never been exposed to anything like this in his life before.

Were Dodi and Diana in love that summer of 1997? I really don't think so. Each found traits in the other that were enticing – a desire for an in-depth and all-consuming relationship, compassion, true interest in the other, and a great chemistry. They were caught up in a typical summer fling, fueled by paparazzi frenzy and heightened by a glamorous and romantic setting.

Much has been written about a potential engagement between Dodi and Diana. Reports have confirmed that Dodi purchased a ring from a jewelry line called *Tell Me Yes*. Dodi's family and staff insist that Dodi planned to propose to the Princess the night they both died.

Diana told both her butler and a few friends that the relationship was not serious, Dodi was spoiling her too much and any ring would be received as a friendship or dinner ring and nothing more.

We'll never know if Dodi did plan to propose on that final evening, but it could help explain why he was so insistent to return to his apartment despite the press buzz when the couple could easily have stayed at the Ritz.

The ring was never found in the car wreck or Dodi's apartment.

What is definitely known is that by the end of the summer, Diana felt the romance had run its course and was more than eager to see her boys and resume her customary routine. She had plans for more humanitarian trips in support of landmine banning, as well as picking up her hectic social schedule.

The plan was for Diana and Dodi to return to London from Sardinia on August 29th. However, Dodi wanted to add one more night to their vacation by detouring to Paris. Diana wasn't too excited about this delay, but was committed to coming back on Dodi's private jet with Al-Fayed's security detail, so she agreed. He sweetened the pot by promising her a celebratory final night dinner at her favourite Parisian restaurant, Chez Benoit.

On August 30th, the pair flew to Paris and were immediately greeted with a ravenous press pack that followed them into the city. Dodi was frustrated with his security team's inability to lose them.

Dodi was excited to detour to Villa Windsor, the French home of the exiled Duke and Duchess of Windsor before their deaths. Mohamed Al-Fayed had purchased the castle and Dodi had hopes of potentially making a holiday home there with Diana. They only stayed for thirty minutes and Diana told a friend a bit later in the day that the place was creepy. It's another sign that Dodi and Diana were not well-matched for the long term. Diana had lived in palaces and castles for almost fifteen years, and was not interested in another drafty old castle, with antiques and ancient royal ghosts.

Once the couple arrived at the Al-Fayed-owned Ritz Hotel, Diana got her hair done and the two relaxed, made phone calls and got ready for their last dinner together. Unknowingly, Diana spoke to a few friends and her sons for the last time.

Stepping out to the car for the short trip to Chez Benoit, the duo was mobbed by photographers on motorcycles. They were closely followed to the restaurant which put a sour note on the start of their evening together.

At the restaurant, Diana was agitated by the crowds of other diners staring at them. Dodi worried that some were going to photograph them. He could see his plans for a romantic tryst were quickly going downhill so he suggested they return to the Ritz for a private dinner in their hotel room.

From this point on that the situation really spun out of control. With only the woefully inadequate Al-Fayed security to protect them, Dodi and Diana were surrounded by flashbulbs, screaming press, an adoring public and almost no protection. There weren't even barricades around the hotel or other venues to keep people back.

By all accounts Dodi was furious with the Parisian paparazzi who were chasing them around the city on motorcycles. There were only two cars and two guards to safeguard the Princess and Dodi. And neither of the protection officers were equipped to deal with issues at this level.

Add to this that Mohamed Al-Fayed was guiding the situation from afar. Neither Dodi nor the bodyguards could make a move without his okay from London.

After a private room service dinner back at the Ritz, Dodi inexplicably decided that the couple should return to Dodi's nearby apartment to spend the night. Whether this was to propose to Diana, to be comfortable with their own things, or some other unknown reason, the two ventured out near midnight to a waiting and insatiable press pack.

Why Dodi didn't just send for his and Diana's

belongings to be brought to the Ritz is an unsolvable mystery. Was it just stubbornness to stick to the plan? Or a frenzy to beat the press at their own game? Or orders from his father? We'll never know.

Diana and Dodi were on the move again. It was Dodi's idea to separate into two separate cars, leaving a decoy at the front of the Ritz, with the second as a getaway for the couple at the back.

According to reports, court evidence and interviews with royal PPOs like Ken Wharfe, this was a crucial mistake. You never split up or leave the principals (Diana and Dodi) with only one protection officer. Security always stays with the people being covered.

We also know that the driver, Henri Paul, was drunk and on prescription painkillers. He was head of security at the Ritz, not a highly-trained royal protection chauffeur. And he verbally taunted the waiting photographers just before the final getaway – not at all professional.

We can only imagine the distress going on in that limousine on the night of August 30th. Adrenalin was pumping, Dodi was angry, the driver was drunk, and the bodyguard was probably frazzled and in over his head. Trevor Rees-Jones was a 29-year old English security guard for the Al-Fayed family. He would never have been trained for such a high-risk operation with such prominent and important passengers as what he faced that night.

As for Diana, we can only conjecture as to her state of mind. She was probably anxious for the safety of the rat pack chasing them so closely on motorbikes. She may have been frustrated with Dodi's constant mind-changing and frenetic movements. Likely, she was wishing she'd never agreed to this side trip and was instead safely in her sitting room at KP with a cup of herbal tea.

It was out of character for Diana not to wear a seat belt.

She usually belted in, and insisted others did. Perhaps she was snuggling close to Dodi for comfort? Thinking it wasn't far to his apartment? No one knows. The most heart-rending tragedy of all is that if she had been wearing a seat belt, she well may have survived the crash.

The unplanned and disorganized movements of the entire day clearly point to the final crash as a calamitous accident, not any form of conspiracy theory. If Diana had been protected by Scotland Yard-trained Personal Protection Officers, none of this zig zagging and last-minute decision-making would have happened.

Instead, the whole day's activities would have been planned out in excruciating detail. Each place on the itinerary would have been walked and driven in advance to perfectly time entrances, exits and backup plans. Rooms would have been swept for bugs, and background checks on anyone coming into contact with Diana would have been performed. Crowd control would have been organized at every location, including the erection of barriers and closing off any entry points that could have compromised the Princess. And most certainly, there would have been more than two cars (one which had previously been in an accident), at least one licensed and experienced driver and plenty of other security. And if any of these protection officers or drivers had any alcohol on his breath, he would have been immediately sent home.

It's ludicrous to think this far-fetched collection of incidents was planned to murder either Dodi or Diana. There were too many unknowns that night, and too much unpredictability with the main players, the press and the public.

It was an appalling accident caused by a drunk driver going too fast, as motorcycle paparazzi chased a limo with Princess Diana and Dodi Fayed through the Alma Tunnel. Ironically, of the four people in the car, the person best equipped to drive in that situation was Diana herself. She had received emergency training in her early years as Princess of Wales, having to evade smoke bombs while driving an obstacle course. And the fifteen years of driving herself around busy London while evading persistent media and photographers had given her excellent concentration and navigation skills.

"Kensington Palace," an unrecognisable voice answered.

"Paul, is that you? It's Nora. Tell me it isn't true. Have you spoken to Diana? She's alright, isn't she?" Her voice shook with fear.

"Yes, it's me. And Nora, no. She's not alright. She was in a crash last night."

"I saw it on the television. A car crash. In Paris. They said Dodi and the driver were killed instantly. And the Princess was seriously injured. She's in hospital. But she's alright? Isn't she Paul?" she repeated almost hysterically as she gripped the phone.

"No, she's not. They, they, they... couldn't save her. They couldn't save her," Paul's voice broke and he started sobbing.

"NO," cried Nora. "Paul, what happened?" She felt as if she'd been punched in the stomach.

"I don't know all the details yet, Nora," he gulped between sobs. "The news is hazy from Paris. But it's true. Buckingham Palace confirmed it. Robert rang me. Dodi and the Princess were out for dinner. They were going back to Mr. Fayed's apartment, I think. The paparazzi were chasing them in a tunnel. And they crashed. You're right that Mr. Fayed and the driver were killed straightaway. I think the bodyguard is seriously injured. The Princess survived the accident and was taken to a local hospital. She had a lot of internal injuries. They tried to save her. But they couldn't. They...they...they couldn't save her." Paul was almost incoherent with grief.

"Paul, they couldn't save her?" Nora asked stupidly. "They couldn't save the Princess of Wales? Why? Why?"

"I don't know, Ma'am. We're still trying to piece everything together. It seems her heart stopped, at least once." He was sobbing uncontrollably now. *"In the end, she died of a broken heart. Oh my god, Ma'am, what are we going to do without her?"* From Diana, A Spencer Forever.

After the Mercedes crashed into the thirteenth pillar in the Alma tunnel, three lives were forever silenced. The driver and Dodi were killed immediately, and the bodyguard Trevor Rees-Jones was critically injured.

Before emergency vehicles arrived, the paparazzi caught up with the royal car, and instantly started snapping photos of everyone inside. None of them called for help or tried to assist the injured Princess or bodyguard. Luckily, none of those pictures have ever been published, but it's still sickening to think of that scene and the disrespect shown to the victims.

A passing doctor stopped and immediately started attending to Diana. Once the ambulances arrived, it was clear that Dodi and Henri Paul were dead. Rees-Jones had to be cut out of the car before being taken to hospital where he underwent weeks and months of surgeries and reconstructions before resuming his life in the U.K.

The French medical team have been severely criticized for taking almost an hour for a 10-15-minute drive to the hospital. It perhaps is not well understood that French ambulances are staffed with doctors (not simply paramedics). In addition to stabilizing the patient on-site, these well-trained doctors have equipment and medication to actually treat patients enroute.

The many official investigations that have been conducted in both France and England have substantiated that the doctors attending Diana worked tirelessly to save her life. She reportedly had at least one heart attack (and perhaps two) from the time of the crash to reaching Pitié-Salpêtrière Hospital. They drove slowly to minimize the risk of another cardiac arrest, also according to protocol.

If they had driven faster and reached the hospital sooner, could Diana have been saved? We'll never know. I like to think the doctors did their absolute best to save the Princess.

Once Diana reached the hospital, she was immediately rushed to surgery, where a team of doctors and specialists fought to stabilize her. Unfortunately, this was not possible. At 4:00 a.m. local time, she was pronounced dead.

The Queen and Prince of Wales were notified at Balmoral Castle. Charles opted not to wake the young princes and waited till morning to break the heart-rending news.

I still remember when I found out that the Princess of Wales was gone. I was staying at a family cottage north of Toronto here in Canada. The morning of August 31st, I went outside to retrieve the daily newspaper from the front step. In massive black letters was the unreal headline, "DIANA DEAD." I couldn't believe it! I immediately turned on the little black and white television to find out what happened. The coverage was sketchy. We cut short our weekend and came back to Toronto where I was glued to the TV, in tears, for that terrible week. Many of you have shared similar experiences about how personally you suffered the death of this amazing woman.

The Queen and royal family were criticized for several blunders that fateful week between Diana's death and her funeral. The first was taking the boys to church business-as-usual that first Sunday morning. No mention of the Princess was made during the sermon, and Harry plaintively asked "Are you sure Mummy is dead?" – presumably confused that life was carrying on without acknowledging his mother's death.

In hindsight, it's understandable that Her Majesty and Prince Charles were in shock. Trying to keep things as normal as possible for William and Harry was their number one priority. This also explains why the entire family (except for Charles who flew to Paris to claim his ex-wife's body), remained at Balmoral.

The family knew they could protect the boys on this private and isolated estate, while keeping them busy and tired with daily outdoor activities like long hikes, fishing and shooting. The Queen and Duke of Edinburgh are after all, William and Harry's grandparents.

As the world awoke to a devastation and grief that was and is still unimaginable, the Windsors and Spencers started to discuss how to handle the funeral of the most famous woman in the world.

The Queen initially believed a private Spencer funeral was the best choice, given that Diana was no longer officially a member of the royal family. At first, she had refused the use of the Queen's Flight for Charles' trip to France but he strongly objected and won this battle. I was sincerely impressed with how the Prince handled this entire set of circumstances. He fought for a classy goodbye to Diana – not easy when your mother is Queen! And remarkable, considering that the Princess was his ex-wife. I'm not sure many men would have handled this with such class and compassion.

Diana's sisters Jane and Sarah flew with Charles to Paris to bring Diana back, along with her trusted butler Paul Burrell. Upon their return, the massive display of open grief on the streets of London persuaded the Spencers that a private ceremony wouldn't be possible, and the royal machine sprang into action.

It was quickly decided that Diana's funeral would be a modified version of the plans for the Queen Mother's service. Codenamed Operation Tay Bridge, it had been rehearsed for 22 years so it could quickly be altered from a state affair to one befitting the mother of a future King. Many of the military aspects were changed (e.g. members of Diana's charities walked behind the funeral cortege), and the Spencers had influence over the planning of the actual service.

Initially, the press and paparazzi were blamed for the accident. Six French photographers (including one incredibly name Romuald Rat) were detained for questioning. The media in both France and England were vilified for their long-term pursuit of any and all pictures of the Princess over the years. Some were openly challenged on the streets of London and public loathing was rampant.

It's important to note that this open revulsion led to at least some of redirected fury against the royal family. The papers were eager for a scapegoat and printed the famous headlines like "Has the House of Windsor Got a Heart?" "Your people are suffering," "Speak to us Ma'am," Show us you care," and "Where is our Queen? Where is our flag?" dominated the news cycle.

Yes, it's true that the flag over Buckingham Palace was not lowered to half-mast. The reason is that the royal standard only flies over a palace when the Queen is in residence. It wouldn't have been appropriate to lower it. It wasn't even flying over the palace at the time. The situation was rectified a few days later when a Union Jack was raised and then lowered to half-mast. The public was appeased.

And yes, the Queen and royal family stayed in Scotland rather than returning to London. They felt, rightly or wrongly, that it was the best place to protect William and Harry. There were valid concerns for the safety of all members of the family. The public outcry against them was palpable, fanned by the negative news coverage.

Buckingham Palace feared the royals might be attacked if they appeared in the open.

This was exposed later in the week when a couple of tests were held – first Princes Andrew and Edward inspected the flowers at Kensington Palace. Then Her Majesty and Prince Philip made a brief and heavily guarded appearance outside the palace. Both forays were successful and the family heaved a sigh of relief.

In a poignant moment, a young girl presented Queen Elizabeth with a small bouquet outside the gates. The Queen asked if the child wanted her to place it on the ever-growing pile for Diana. The youngster replied, "No, they are for you, Ma'am." It was a small incident, but confirmed that the people still supported the monarchy.

The new Prime Minister, Tony Blair, was instrumental in helping the royal family manage this crisis in a human way. He went on camera almost immediately after the accident, giving a voice to the nation's anguish, coining the phrase, "The People's Princess." He encouraged the Queen to come to London sooner than the funeral, which she did. He influenced her unprecedented live speech from Buck House the night before the funeral. He worked with Prince Charles to ensure the public had as much access to pay respects to the Princess as possible.

People waited in line for up to twelve hours to sign Books of Condolences, and many more books had to be added. Flower shops sold out as blankets of flowers, tributes, candles, teddy bears, notes and letters surrounded the gates of Buckingham and Kensington Palaces. Tearful strangers comforted each other on the streets of London as they tried to make sense of the impossible catastrophe. This was almost unthinkable for the reserved and detached British people.

The funeral was set for Saturday, September 6th. As the week wore on, arrangements rapidly progressed. The route was extended as a million people were expected to line the cortege route from Kensington Palace to Westminster Abbey. Two huge screens were erected to broadcast the Westminster Abbey service live in Hyde Park. By Wednesday, people were already camping out, holding vigils for Diana.

Back in Scotland, returning from Crathie Kirk, Charles stopped the car at the Balmoral gates. He, William and Harry looked at the flowers and messages that had been left. The images were painful to watch – two young boys distraught and bewildered by it all.

Earl Charles Spencer decided that Diana would be buried on an island at Althorp to keep her away from prying eyes. He labored over his eulogy, which would transpire to be a searing attack on the press and royal family.

Not only the Windsors and Spencers were grieving. The Al-Fayed family buried their beloved Dodi, and Mohamed was starting to claim conspiracy theories. Initial police reports were indicating that the driver Henri Paul had blood alcohol in his system, and the blame began to shift from the paparazzi to the intoxicated chauffeur.

Over a million people paid their respects on September 6th as Diana, Princess of Wales made her final journey from her Kensington Palace home to Westminster Abbey. She had spent her final night at KP, with loyal butler Paul Burrell holding an all-night vigil over her coffin.

At 9:00 a.m. the royal standard-draped casket left Kensington Palace for the almost two-hour journey to the Abbey. It was eerily silent in London, except for the minute-tolling of the Abbey bell, and the wailing of the grieving souls.

As the cortege passed Buckingham Palace, the Queen, standing by the West Gate with other members of the royal family, bowed her head. This was a fitting mark of respect from a reigning sovereign for a beloved daughter-in-law.

Gasps of sorrow pierced the air as the mourners noticed an envelope simply marked "Mummy" atop a flower display. It was incredibly moving. But the agony wasn't over yet.

Audible reaction and tears from the crowd punctuated the atmosphere as Diana's sons, aged 15 and 12, fell into step behind the coffin alongside their father, Earl Spencer, and Prince Philip. Who of us can ever forget that sight? We still remember it to this day, and the feelings of distress and sympathy we felt for those poor boys.

An estimated 2.5 billion people around the world watched the Princess' funeral, making it one of the biggest televised events in history.

The funeral began at precisely 11:00 a.m. Diana's favourite hymn was played – I Vow to Thee my Country. Nora recalled it had also been played at her wedding, fifteen years ago. Heartbreaking.

Diana's sisters each faltered through readings and the Prime Minister read from the bible. Sir Elton John performed Candle in the Wind but had changed the lyrics for the Princess of Wales and how her candle would never burn out. How fitting, thought Nora. Diana had always felt a kinship to Marilyn Monroe for whom the song had originally been written. What an appalling coincidence that they had both been taken too soon at age thirty-six. Goodbye England's Rose seemed so right. She didn't know how Elton got through it. She herself was weeping.

But the biggest shock was when Diana's brother, Earl Spencer strode to the pulpit to read the eulogy. It was nothing less than a fiery attack on the royal family. Gasps of breath followed one after the other as the Earl beat mercilessly on.

"She would want us today to pledge ourselves to protecting her beloved boys William and Harry from a similar fate, and I do this here Diana on your behalf. We will not allow them to suffer the anguish that used regularly to drive you to tearful despair.

And beyond that, on behalf of your mother and sisters, I pledge that we, your blood family, will do all we can to continue the imaginative way in which you were steering these two exceptional young men so that their souls are not simply immersed by duty and tradition but can sing openly as you planned."

The Queen stared ahead in stony silence as Harry cried. But the Earl was not finished.

"I would like to end by thanking God for the small mercies he has shown us at this dreadful time. For taking Diana at her most beautiful and radiant and when she had joy in her private life. Above all we give thanks for the life of a woman I am so proud to be able to call my sister, the unique, the complex, the extraordinary and irreplaceable Diana whose beauty, both internal and external, will never be extinguished from our minds."

His voice splintered as he kneeled before his sister's coffin. The Abbey went silent.

Suddenly, a rumbling started, almost like the sound of rain pounding on the roof. Nora looked at Mary questioningly. What could be happening? Then, it hit her. It was clapping. Large video screens had been placed in Hyde and Regent Parks so that the public could watch the funeral. They'd hung on the Earl's every word. Applause rolled up the aisle of the Abbey in a thunderous wave. Soon, everyone began clapping, a spontaneous outburst of emotion for the Princess. Nora doubted anyone had ever applauded a royal funeral at Westminster Abbey before. You were never one to do it by the rule book, Diana, Nora smiled to herself.

As the applause died down, the casket was raised again and carried down the aisle where a moment of silence was observed.

Then, the coffin was raised into the hearse to make its journey to Diana's final resting place at Althorp. The Spencers had truly reclaimed her in death. She was to be buried on the estate on an island in an ornamental lake known as The Round Oval.

Nora found out later that as the hearse and its guard slowly drove northward, people lining the route tossed bouquets of flowers continuously at the car and windshield. At many points, the car had to stop to remove flowers for visibility and safety's sake. The unearthly silence of London followed the procession to its final destination. Whilst the hearse drove to Northamptonshire, the Spencers and the Windsors rode the royal train for the interment. Given the Earl's eulogy, that couldn't have been a comfortable journey.

The final committal was private with only the families, and Paul Burrell, in attendance. From Diana, A Spencer Forever

And so ends the story of Diana's final residence – Kensington Palace. Her rooms there were unoccupied until her son Prince William, his wife Kate and their children had these apartments renovated. It is now their London home.

Significant Events that happened at Kensington Palace

- Charles and Diana move into Kensington Palace as their official London residence: 1982
- William Arthur Philip Louis Wales is born at St. Mary's Hospital: June 1982
- Henry Charles Albert David Wales is born at St. Mary's Hospital: September 1984
- Charles resumed his affair with Camilla Parker-Bowles: 1986
- Diana begins affair with Major James Hewitt: 1986
- Diana conquers her bulimia: 1989
- Diana hugs an AIDS patient: 1991
- Diana's father, Earl Johnnie Spencer dies: 1992
- The Duke and Duchess of York separate: 1992
- *Diana, Her True Story* published: 1992
- *Squidgygate* tape exposed: 1992
- Charles and Diana separation announced at the British House of Parliament: 1992

- Diana makes KP her primary residence: 1993
- *Camillagate* tape exposed: 1993
- Diana announces her withdrawal from public life: 1993
- Charles reveals his affair during Jonathon Dimbleby interview: 1994
- Diana fights back with her own secret *Panorama* interview with Martin Bashir: 1995
- Diana begins secret relationship with Dr. Hasnat Khan: 1995
- Charles and Diana are officially divorced: 1996
- Diana gets involved with global landmine issue: 1996
- Diana auctions off 79 of her formal dresses at Christie's auction in New York: 1997
- Diana breaks ties with Hasnat Khan: 1997
- Diana spends vacation time aboard the Al-Fayed yacht & home with Dodi Fayed: 1997
- Diana dies in car crash in a Paris tunnel: 1997
- Diana's coffin rests for one last night before the funeral: 1997
- Funeral of Diana, Princess of Wales: 1997

In Her Own Words

"Just look at all these dresses. How many ballgowns do you think there are in this room? Each one of these is a memory and an old friend, but now is the time to sell them all." Diana, Princess of Wales.

Kensington Palace Today

KP is open for tourists on a wide basis. Located in the prestigious Kensington district of London, it's easy to find. It's about a fifteen-minute walk from the High Street Kensington tube station, and you can shop Kensington High Street before or after your visit. Keen royal-watchers can spot the Marks & Spencer and McDonald's frequented by Diana and her sons.

Many visitors are surprised and disappointed that Diana's apartments are not open for viewing, so be prepared. Most of the exhibits date back to the time of Queen Victoria, who lived here before she was Queen, and King William and Queen Mary II. You can tour their royal apartments.

Not open to the public are the offices and residences of The Duke and Duchess of Gloucester, The Duke and Duchess of Kent and Prince and Princess Michael of Kent. Princess Eugenie lives at Ivy Cottage on the property with her husband Jack Brooksbank.

There's usually an exhibit on that is worth seeing – often some of Diana's gowns. Make a reservation for afternoon tea at The Orangery. In my opinion, it's the best in London. And spend a few hours walking the Kensington Palace Gardens and pond with stops at the Diana, Princess of Wales playground and memorial fountain.

Plan for a day to see it all. Visit hrp.org.uk/kensington-palace/#gs.u2gmdi for opening times and visitor information.

TWELVE

Spencer House

London, England

Spencer House is not an official royal residence but I wanted to include it because it's a centuries-old sliver of Spencer history. It is a Georgian mansion overlooking Green Park, and a short walk from Buckingham Palace. It is one of the only great London eighteenth-century town houses to survive intact. Originally designed by John Vardy, it was conceived as a showcase of classical design by the first Earl Spencer in 1756. John Spencer wanted a lavish London residence for his young bride, Georgiana – Diana's great-great-great-great-great Aunt.

It has been seen as a monument to true love between the Earl and his Countess, who were prominent figures in London society. During their lifetime Spencer House was often the setting for lavish entertainments. Boasting white Greek columns and neoclassical details made it an imposing presence overlooking Green Park. The Ritz Hotel is a stone's throw away from the magnificent estate.

It has undergone numerous renovations by the original owner, the architect Henry Holland, and many Spencer Earls since then, but still maintains its architectural integrity and historic significance. In addition to a dozen or so bedrooms and full servant's quarters, the main floor is a showpiece that includes a grand Dining Room, Music Room, Great Room and Diana's favorite – the Palm Room.

"Don't you just love it here? I can feel the spirits of our ancestors gliding through the halls. I can almost hear Georgiana's skirts rustling through the doorways as she greeted her guests." Diana studied the room with a dreamy expression on her face. She loved Spencer House and it had been her idea to dine here tonight. She found the romantic story of the first Earl and his wife enthralling.

Her sister Sarah snorted. "Diana, will you never cease to have starry-eyed ideas? That was centuries ago. This old relic is alright, I suppose. But it's just a house, after all."

"Sod off, Sarah," chided Jane good-naturedly. "It is a grand old place and one of the only remaining 18th century aristocratic homes left in London. I agree with Diana. I'm proud it's in the Spencer family." Jane was ever the peacemaker.

She and Sarah sipped on Pimms whilst Diana helped herself to coffee from the tea tray.

Diana carried on, without seeming to have noticed Sarah's barbed remark.

"It's really a lovely old place. Remember the stories Grandmother Spencer used to tell us about how during the Blitz in World War II, all the precious paintings and sculptures were moved to Althorp for safekeeping? Even the doorframes and fireplace marble were dismantled and sent. It's looking much better since the recent restoration – truly glorious." The *Princess smiled.* From Diana, A Spencer Forever

Famous visitors to Spencer House include Queen Victoria, King George V (as Duke of York) and the present Queen.

Spencer House Today

Spencer House is open Sundays only, so be sure to check before you book. It borders Green Park and is within walking distance of both Clarence House and Buckingham Palace, but advance bookings are required. It's a bit tricky to find. I suggest you walk south from Green Park tube station along the edge of the park. On your left, you'll see the large white Spencer House frontage facing the park. There's a small gate to the left of it which will take you through a small passageway. The entrance to Spencer House is on your right.

The official guided tour is about an hour long, and you'll see all the principal state rooms: Ante-Room, Library, Dining Room, Palm Room, Music Room, Lady Spencer's Room, and the Great Painted Room. The guides are knowledgeable and will happily share the history of the house and Spencer family.

As with the Althorp ancestral home, Spencer House is filled with priceless antiques and art, first edition books and valuable tapestries and sculptures.

It's a pretty tour and you'll gain lots of insight into the illustrious and long-standing Spencer history. You could potentially combine it with a visit to Clarence House,

Buckingham Palace or the Buck House Shop for a full day of royal adventures in the heart of London. Definitely worth it! Visit <u>spencerhouse.co.uk</u> for opening times and visitor information.

Diana, Princess of Wales was only thirty-six when she died. Her sons were just fifteen and twelve. Although she had accomplished an extraordinary amount in her short life, her potential to make even more of an impact was silenced forever. Luckily, her sons William and Harry and their children are her living legacy. She would be so proud.

Author's Note

If you enjoyed *At Home with Diana*, I hope you'll want to explore my Diana Spencer trilogy. These historically-based novels tell Princess Diana's complete story from her first meeting with Prince Charles through her extraordinary life up to her tragic death in 1997. See history come to life with Diana's distinctive perspective. Visit your local amazon on-line store to order kindle or paperback versions today.

The complete Diana Spencer Series:
Diana, A Spencer in Love
Diana, A Spencer in Turmoil
Diana, A Spencer Forever

To learn more about Princess Diana, upcoming events and to sign up for my newsletter, please visit my website at **debstratas.com.** Please join my **princessdianabooks** Facebook group. You can also follow me on Twitter at **@debstratas** and **deb stratas** on Instagram. I'd love to hear from you!

Feedback is a gift. Please return to the amazon page where you bought this book to leave a review and brief comment. I thank you so much!

Deb Stratas

Printed in Great Britain
by Amazon